# FLORA

The Graphic Book of the Garden

GUY BARTER

Illustrated by
SAM FALCONER

## PLANNING

## PLANTING

## CHOOSING

## VEGETABLES & HERBS

## FRUIT & VINES

## PRACTICALITIES

# Introduction

Gardening is, or at least becomes, a work of joy and pleasure. It is rather easy to get bogged down in details of design, culture and problems, which although important and unavoidable from time to time, can undermine the motivation and spirit of the gardener. By setting these details in pictures that entrance the reader it is easier to convey the creativity and the sheer delight of growing plants and arranging them in a garden that makes gardening the fascinating and rewarding activity it is.

Words are notoriously inadequate to capture the craft and art of gardening and photographs unfortunately cannot always capture the broad sense of gardening principles, but pictures can do these things.

At the outset there are many apparently complex problems. We have addressed these in a series of manageable sections; aspect, slope, climate and light or shade and the effect these have on plants.

Once we have addressed these, there come the compromises all but the most fortunate must make in fitting all that a gardener might want in their plot; paths, patio, greenhouse, fences, walls and perhaps even a conservatory. Children perhaps derive special benefit from access to a garden and their needs ought to be considered.

Difficult sites – very narrow and awkward shapes, for example – can make gardeners downhearted, but in fact with a good eye and generous planting, awkward sites can often be made the most charming gardens.

Some people are happy for their garden to evolve as it grows and they add to their stock of plants, but others prefer to have a coherent garden from the outset and for these basic elements of design are covered. In truth it is usually more pleasing and avoids moving plants later if design principles remain somewhere in mind whenever new plants are introduced.

With the fundamentals out of the way, it is time to plant. Gardeners can be forgiven for being overwhelmed (there are 75,000 plants listed in the *RHS Plant Finder*, for example), so the plant groups are illustrated in detail from lawns and hedges to climbers and trees.

Some plants are understandably popular, Japanese maples, roses and wisteria for example, and most gardeners will want to use these freely. But plant groups such as annuals, herbaceous plants and bulbs are invaluable and guidance in making the best use of these flexible (and relatively inexpensive) plants has been extensively illustrated. Container plants both indoors and out are vital parts of modern gardens and indeed smaller gardens are often transformed by the use of potted plants so these too are covered.

Growing your own fruit and vegetables remains an extremely popular activity, with even small gardens accommodating a fruiting fence of squash and cucumbers, a wigwam of climbing beans and troughs of salads, a bed of strawberries or a potted blueberry or better, two, since they are best if cross pollinated. Few have space to grow swathes of veg and groves of fruit, so naturally getting the most from limited space (not to mention time and energy) has guided us here.

Tucked away at the back of most books are the practicalities: fertilizer, pests, weeds and perhaps less problematically composting and making new plants, which can easily confuse or even intimidate or weary gardeners. It is true we too have put these at the back, but we have lavished care on these so they are far from an afterthought but rather an essential part of the skills and knowledge that gardeners can relish.

# Planning

# Aspect

Whether a garden, or part of a garden such as a wall, faces north, east, south or west greatly affects what will grow best in that site. South- and west-facing are generally warmer than north- and east-facing gardens or borders.

**South-facing** gardens clearly get much more light than those facing north, but of course slope is very significant too. South-facing slopes are especially warm and well lit; with north-facing ones the opposite applies.

**East- and west**-facing gardens are neither as warm as south-facing nor as cold as north-facing ones. East usually means colder, even though the sun rises in the east, as the night chill is deeper and slow to lift. In frosty periods the sudden thawing of frozen plant parts such as flower buds can be damaging.

**West-facing** is not quite as disadvantageous as east, as the setting sun is typically more warming. Although warming in the morning is slower than for east-facing walls, this means that frozen plant material will thaw more gradually, reducing plant damage.

North-facing slopes can be planted with evergreens and woodland plants, making charming shady, cool, summer outdoor spaces and tranquil winter walks.

W

Pruning or even removal of trees to the south, west or east of the garden can alter the exposure and allow aspect full expression.

N

S

E

Gardens or parts of gardens especially favoured by aspect are often called 'sun-traps'. Tender plants can often be 'chanced' in sheltered, sun-trap areas.

A compass or smartphone will indicate north, and if you stand with your back to the walls of buildings you can immediately see which way the garden faces.

# Slope

Water of course runs down slopes, and gardens with slopes are usually well drained, and even drought-prone if the slope faces south. Where the soil is rich in clay and liable to remain wet for long periods after rain, a slope is often the only place where drought-tolerant plants (which often struggle in wet soil) will thrive.

Sometimes gardeners have to 'follow the flow' and build ponds at the base of slopes. Such ponds look very natural and appropriate. Ponds perched on higher terrain look rather forced. The look of natural springs can also be emulated with a suitable water feature where water arises in a 'hillside spring', natural or pumped, and flows to the pond.

Both water and cold air can be intercepted and diverted. Fences, hedges or climber-clad trellis across the slope can deflect cold air to the side or hinder water, allowing it to soak in.

Shrubs that make good cover for slopes include heathers for sunny acid soils, those that have a protective basket-like twig structure such as snowberries (*Symphoricarpos* species) and low-growing evergreens including Californian lilac (*Ceanothus* species).

Another solution is to plant only **very hardy subjects** with good water-logging tolerance at the base of slopes, such as dogwoods (*Cornus*), elders (*Sambucus*), poplars (*Populus*) and willows (*Salix*). Unfortunately not only can water collect at the base of slopes, creating wet conditions that promote root diseases, but also cold air flows downhill and frosts are more frequent and deeper at the base of a slope. Points for cold air are known as frost pockets.

**Timber decks** can be built projecting from slopes, perhaps offering tree-top views and ferny caves below. The good airflow associated with elevation keeps down the slippery algae that can make decks unpleasant and potentially hazardous.

**Low-maintenance plants** are usually a high priority, as pruning and weeding on gradients is less readily accomplished than on the level. Many public gardens seek to save labour by making 'horizontal hedges' using plants such as beech (*Fagus sylvatica*) and cherry laurel (*Prunus laurocerasus*). These are closely planted and trimmed mechanically each summer to make a level leafy surface that provides cover all year. Beech treated in this way holds its autumn leaves until spring.

# Shelter

Wind stresses plants through bending and chafing, greater and more rapid variations in temperature, and speeding up water-loss from the foliage. Wind may flow evenly over flat areas but in gardens every obstruction, such as trees, shrubs, buildings and fences, diverts the wind up and sideways, inducing turbulence. These obstacles have to be taken into account when designing shelter, as has the direction of the prevailing wind.

Shelter from wind can greatly improve plant growth and health, as well as the earliness and quality of produce and blooms. Yet while providing ample shelter has many benefits, there are several factors to consider. Trees, or belts of trees (shelterbelts), shrubberies, trellis, hedges, and fences or walls take up space and cast considerable shade. Walls are costly but long-lasting, while fences are less expensive but less durable. Hedges and especially trees take time to grow, and also use soil moisture and nutrients.

Shelter can also provide privacy, but views and vistas might be incompatible with good shelter and difficult choices might have to be made.

Shelter then is often a case of the minimum required for the intended planting. This can range from thick shelter, perhaps even a shelterbelt, for fruit trees (to allow good pollination and avoid fruit being blown from the branches before harvest) or little or no shelter for wind-tolerant heather borders to coastal sites where the view is valued, despite the windy conditions.

**Solid barriers** such as fence panels, walls and tightly pruned evergreen hedges block airflow, and the resulting turbulence can be almost as damaging as exposure to uninhibited breezes. On the other hand, solid barriers provide the best privacy. Trellis on top of solid fences and walls will filter airflow and reduce turbulence. Wind also works its way around the ends of shelter, so corners of gardens need particular care.

**The best shelter** for plants filters airflow and reduces the wind speed without turbulence. A closely clipped but thin deciduous hedge of beech or hornbeam works in this way. This can still provide a good level of privacy by masking any movement that can be seen through the hedge.

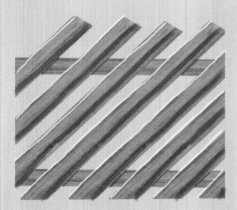

When it comes to **fences,** porous types give best protection if they are about 50 per cent permeable. Lath (wooden strip) fences with laths separated by gaps are especially useful in seaside gardens.

**'Hit** and **miss' fences** where wooden battens are nailed on each side of rails with gaps on each side so that they partially overlap, thus leaving vertical gaps, provide privacy and also slow the wind without causing turbulence.

# Walls and boundaries

Hedges, walls, fences and trellis usually delineate the garden perimeter and divide up the garden internally. They also have a role in providing shelter, privacy and security. However, their effectiveness at reducing noise is limited, as it is not possible to block out noise from upper windows, up-hill sources or aircraft.

Barriers should be thick enough so noise cannot penetrate, and also high enough to prevent too much noise 'curling' over the top. Height, however, is a nuisance in gardens as it can cast shade and if over 2m (6½ft) can require planning permission. Using a double set of panels or special 'acoustic fencing' is an option to reduce noise infiltration. Walls are sufficiently dense to absorb any noise they do not reflect.

Adding planting such as climbers, wall shrubs and vertical growing systems used to make 'green walls' will enhance the sound-absorbing properties of walls and fences.

Hedges are probably the best boundary on the grounds of cost and environmental friendliness, but they do need upkeep, take time to grow and are seldom satisfactory in shade. For this reason fences of panels or featherboards of timber treated with wood preservatives are a common choice for providing privacy and shelter. Panels require very strong supporting posts set in concrete.

Other environmentally sustainable fences include **hurdles** made from coppiced ash, hazel, sweet chestnut and willow trees. In coppicing, the tree is cut to near ground level at intervals of about 10–15 years to stimulate the growth of long, straight poles.

Variations on this include **chestnut paling** fences, which are a good way of providing short-term security while hedges grow, and also lightweight willow screens.

**Dry hedges** are barriers of twiggy sticks laid horizontally between upright stakes to make a dense 40-cm/16-in wide 'hedge'.

**The smaller** a **garden** is, the more the boundaries eat into the space available for planting. Walls, although expensive, offer the best 'microclimate' of shelter and, depending on aspect, of warmth and light. Unfortunately they require substantial foundations or footings of concrete if they are to resist wind pressure, and this can interfere with the roots of climbers and shrubs planted against them. Planting 50cm/20in out from the wall allows good rooting and also puts the plant in moist soil outside the 'rain shadow' of the wall.

Fences **do not require foundations** and cast less 'rain shadow'. Rain runs down into the soil, where it is accessible to roots growing under the fence.

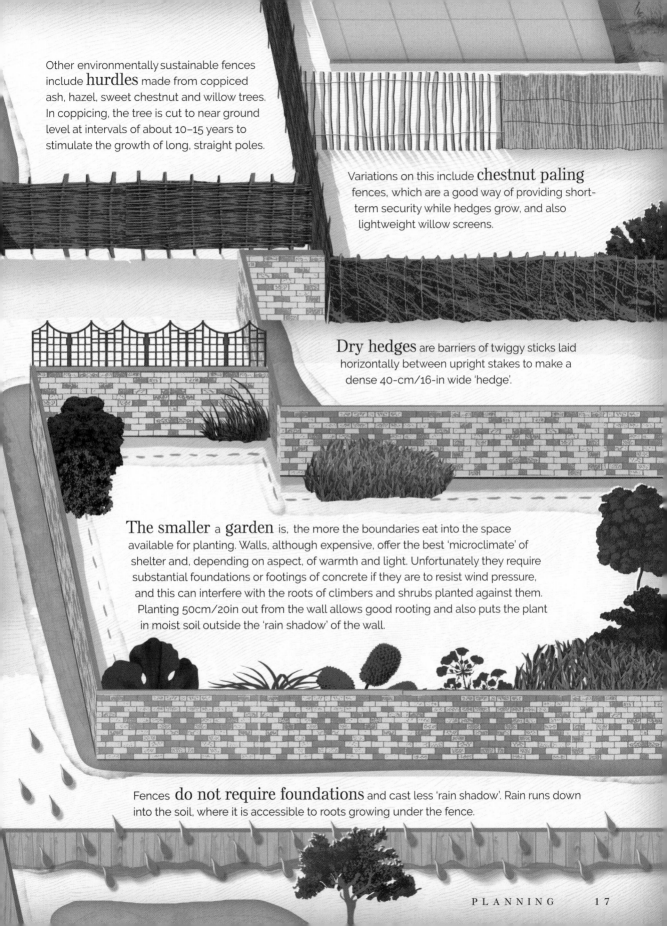

# Space

Space, for many people, is tight and often in awkward shapes. However, there are ways to make the most of what your space offers and create a flourishing garden. Happily, plants seem unaware of space and just grow until they fill it.

**Tiny spaces** such as balconies and the outdoor stairwells down to basement flats can be planted.

**Balconies** can be very windy, which dries plants out, especially if they are also sunny. Drought-resistant succulents and Mediterranean plants including herbs such as lavender and rosemary are ideal. Naturally pots will be needed for planting, and as weight can soon accumulate it is best to use a lightweight soil-free potting medium with perlite to avoid overloading structures.

The same goes for **roof gardens** – wind and sun dries plants out and although large volumes of potting medium would provide a reserve of moisture, weight can be an issue. If pots have to be kept small, an automatic watering system can be used. Trellis and screening will slow wind speed on balconies and roofs.

**Shady balconies** and stairwells are less prone to drying out and foliage plants, especially those tolerant of shade, are a good choice.

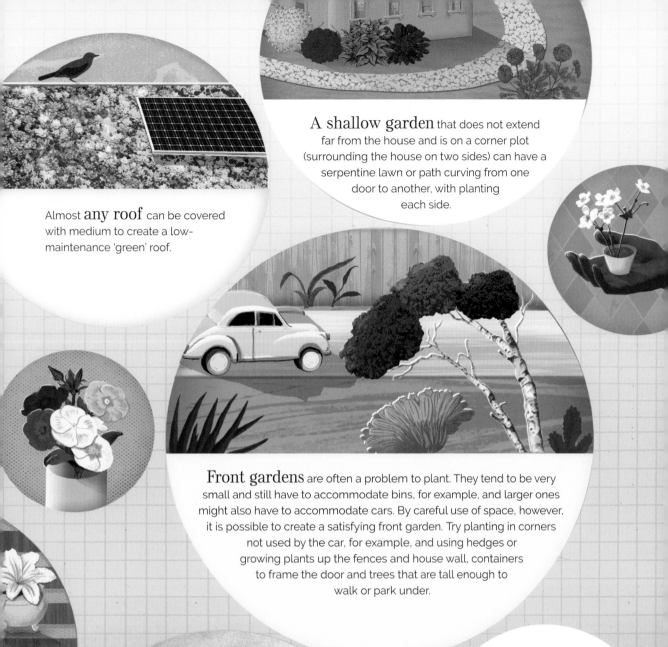

A **shallow garden** that does not extend far from the house and is on a corner plot (surrounding the house on two sides) can have a serpentine lawn or path curving from one door to another, with planting each side.

Almost **any roof** can be covered with medium to create a low-maintenance 'green' roof.

**Front gardens** are often a problem to plant. They tend to be very small and still have to accommodate bins, for example, and larger ones might also have to accommodate cars. By careful use of space, however, it is possible to create a satisfying front garden. Try planting in corners not used by the car, for example, and using hedges or growing plants up the fences and house wall, containers to frame the door and trees that are tall enough to walk or park under.

Some **lucky people** have more space than they can realistically handle. One way to tackle this is to buy a very big ride-on mower.

**Long, narrow** gardens offer the intriguing possibility of a series of rooms with a long view from back door to garden gate, or a curve of sweeping lawn down the middle. Arranging paths to be barely visible by taking them down the base of the fence or hedge helps to avoid making them seem narrow and short.

# Light

Light is fundamental for plant growth because it powers photosynthesis, the formation of sugar from water and carbon dioxide in the atmosphere, without which there would be virtually no life on earth.

Gardens are peculiar in that light levels vary greatly within a short distance. Choosing plants that match the available light is important as light levels cannot be enhanced in the way that water and fertility can be manipulated. Indoors, though, artificial light can be provided at a price.

Another very important gardening aspect of light quality is its relative richness in red light. Sunlight contains more or less equal amounts of red and the longer wavelength, far red light. Red light is absorbed by leaves but the far red light passes through. Plants can detect and measure this with a sophisticated molecule called phytochrome, and adjust their growth to the conditions. Little red light and high far red light tells shade-intolerant plants that they are shaded, and in response they grow long and thin (etiolated) towards better light.

Light levels and day length also vary by latitude – the relative position of a garden to the Equator and the poles.

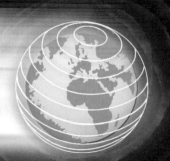

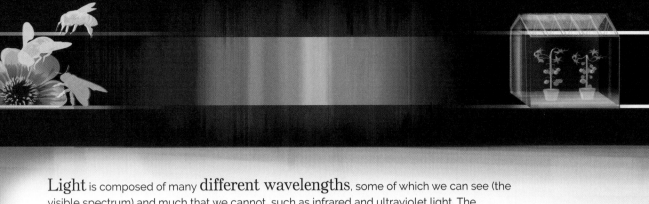

**Light** is composed of many **different wavelengths**, some of which we can see (the visible spectrum) and much that we cannot, such as infrared and ultraviolet light. The chlorophyll molecules in plants capture a limited range of wavelengths, and the remaining light is not used for photosynthesis, although it may be significant in other ways. Insects can perceive ultraviolet light, and infrared is important in glasshouses, where shorter wavelengths can enter to warm the contents but the warmed contents re-emit longer wavelength light that cannot pass through glass and remains trapped within.

**Day length**, or more accurately the duration of night, is another facet of light of great importance to gardeners. This varies by season and can affect plants' flowering. Plants can measure day length very well and use the length of darkness by night to regulate flowering. Short-day plants such as chrysanthemums and poinsettias flower in autumn by nature, as days get shorter, while long-day plants such as hardy geraniums flower in summer when the days are longer.

Day length also controls other plant activities. Bulb formation in onions, for example, only occurs once the **days become long**, while in autumn leaves fall off deciduous trees and shrubs. The leaves of a particular species all fall more or less simultaneously in the same geographic region.

# Climate

Climates are determined by latitude and hence the level of solar radiation, with most heat being absorbed in the tropics. This heat might, in a non-rotating world, move north-south by convection of air and sea water. Although the heat absorbed in the tropics is a fundamental driver of climate, the rotation of the planet is also important.

**Due to the** west-to-east rotation of the earth, winds are deflected to the right so move in a westerly direction in the northern hemisphere and to the left in the southern hemisphere. Winds therefore tend to blow from the south-west in the northern hemisphere and north-west in the southern hemisphere, leading to significantly wet regions on the windward side of continents, including Atlantic Europe, in the middle latitudes.

Climate is of course **seasonal**, even in most of the tropics, with varying warmth and rainfall that very much dictates what plants can be grown.

The wind drives ocean currents as well, such as the North Atlantic Drift (or Gulf Stream) that warms Atlantic Europe.

One widely used climate classification system, the **Köppen system**, lists five climate types:

**A**  Tropical Moist Climates where the climate is always hot

**B**  Dry Climates or deserts

**C**  Moist Mid-Latitude Climates with mild winters – usually coastal

**D**  Moist Mid-Latitude Climates with cold winters – usually continental

**E**  Polar Climates

Although the climate sets broad boundaries, the day-to-day weather can be highly variable for reasons that remain poorly understood, as can be seen in the lack of precision in weather forecasts.

Plants from cold climates will only be capable of flowering when they have measured a certain amount of cold (expressed as hours between certain critical temperatures, typically 2–12°C/ 36–54°F).

Naturally latitude also determines climate, from the hot equatorial regions with equal length of day and night to the poles where there is little winter daytime and virtually no night in summer.

Bulbs from climates with hot dry summers and mild moist winters, cyclamen and nerines for example, go underground for summer to avoid heat damage and desiccation, and send up leaves only in winter.

**Winter cold** is a limiting factor, with plants from areas near the poles taking extreme measures to protect themselves from the damaging ice crystals that form when plants freeze. Three mechanisms are used: dissolving sugars in their sap to lower the freezing point, as in adding salt to roads before frosts; by removing materials from their sap that will allow the sap to get cold without freezing; and by placing water from cells in conductive vessels where it can freeze without rupturing cells and internal membranes.

# Microclimate

With climate setting a broad definition of the growing environment, and weather covering the day-to-day variations, there still remain small-scale factors covering the actual experience of plants that apply locally and involve soil type, exposure to winds, light levels and warmth.

These factors can start outside the garden, such as exposure to wind from nearby sea or plains, or conversely shelter provided by a hill positioned to windward. When the hills are high and to the west they intercept rain clouds, forcing them to rise and shed water as they cool with altitude. In the western USA inland deserts are caused by the high mountains of the coastal ranges.

High land can also be a source of cold air in winter, and especially in spring during frosty nights. This cold air is relatively dense and may flow downhill, accumulating in low-lying areas, subjecting plants in these positions to deep and prolonged cold. The depth of chilled air is often sufficient to affect a tall tree.

However, even very small sites can have a significantly enhanced climate for plants. A sheltered sunny angle in a fence or wall may allow a much more tender plant to grow than would be expected to thrive elsewhere in the garden. Alternatively a north-facing dark angle in a fence or wall cries out for ferns and woodland plants that might scorch and dry out in less protected spots in summer. On the other hand, those north-facing patches can be dreadful frost pockets in winter, seldom thawing out for weeks on end.

Urban areas are warmer than nearby rural areas, and in fact large cities are significantly warmer than open country, meaning that even tender plants, bedding cyclamen for example, can survive winter in favourable spots .

South-facing walls are excellent places for a warmer and sunnier microclimate that reflects heat and light onto plants, and the warmed masonry radiates heat by night. Apricots, figs, nectarines and peaches are traditional plants for these places.

Sheltering trees and hedges greatly reduce wind stress and enhance early-flowering plants such as irises and peonies, which may be spoilt by wind. They help early vegetables reach maturity sooner, including lettuces and cauliflowers, and also benefit fruit trees, whose flowers may pollinate poorly if windy conditions at blossom-time adversely affect insects.

# Hardiness

Hardiness essentially means the degree of cold that plants can withstand – to put it another way, how well a plant stands up to a factor of the local climate that limits plant growth. In some climates this may be heat or drought, but in the temperate regions it usually means cold.

Hardiness ratings to **help gardeners** choose plants suited to their conditions have been developed most notably by the United States Department of Agriculture (USDA) and, as shown below, by the Royal Horticultural Society in the UK:

**Hardiness** is not a set property but is modified by other factors related to weather and indeed culture – plants lavishly watered and fed are less hardy than ones that have been denied this special care, but they will have grown very much faster than those treated in a more rigorous way.

Tender plants are typically sickly below 12°C/54°F often because their cell membranes fail to function properly at these low temperatures. If these plants freeze they will be killed. Therefore, greenhouse protection in winter is essential.

**H1a** Warmer than 15°C/59°F.
Heated glasshouse – tropical

**H1b** Warmer than 10–15°C/50–59°F.
Heated glasshouse – subtropical

**H1c** Warmer than 5–10°C/41–50°F.
Heated glasshouse – warm temperate

**H2** Warmer than 1–5°C/34–41°F.
Cool or frost-free glasshouse – tender

In the **spring** plants grown in greenhouses suffer damage if exposed to outdoor temperatures, and it is customary to harden them off by exposing them to gradually increasing doses of cold and wind. This can be done by placing them in a structure such as cold frame, an intermediate between the rigours of outdoors and the shelter of the greenhouse.

**Stressing** or hardening plants to one stress factor, say drought, can also induce resilience to cold, so 'drying off' container plants as autumn approaches can stiffen their resistance to the coming cold.

**Hardy plants** can survive the level of frost expected in the garden concerned. Typically this means they can survive frosts down to about -15°C/5°F, which is the extreme found in the UK. Such plants may not be hardy in Canada or Scandinavia.

**Half-hardy** plants may often survive, especially if a suitable microclimate can be found for them, but it is generally safer to protect them in a greenhouse over winter, or raise afresh each spring from seeds or cuttings overwintered in a greenhouse.

**H3** Warmer than -5 to 1°C/23–34°F. Unheated glasshouse or mild winter – half-hardy (hardy in coastal or mild areas)

**H4** Warmer than -10 to -5°C/14–23°F. Average winter – hardy

**H5** Warmer than -15 to -10°C/5–14°F. Cold winter – hardy

**H6** Warmer than -20 to -15°C/-4 to 5°F . Very cold winter – hardy (hardy northern Europe)

**H7** Colder than -20°C/-4°F – bone hardy

# Drainage

Too much water can be as bad as too little. Surplus water excludes air from the soil, leading to suffocation of roots and also the suppression of beneficial organisms that contribute to healthy and productive soil. Naturally, bog gardens are slightly different and here drainage might need to be impaired rather than enhanced.

## Sometimes
new-build homes lie on soil so damaged by building machinery that the natural drainage has been seriously compromised. Homebuyers with a wish to garden should be alert to this possibility when considering property in low-lying areas.

## Waterlogging through
rainfall usually occurs in winter. As the soil is cold at this season, plant roots are dormant and are not susceptible to harm either from drowning or by diseases associated with wet soil, especially the potentially highly destructive fungus-like organisms *Pythium* and *Phytophthora*.

**Farmers** often claim that drains are the most profitable thing they plant, but they have access to ditches and streams to carry surplus water away. Domestic premises often lack anywhere for the water to go and the fact that this may also apply to neighbouring properties compounds the problem.

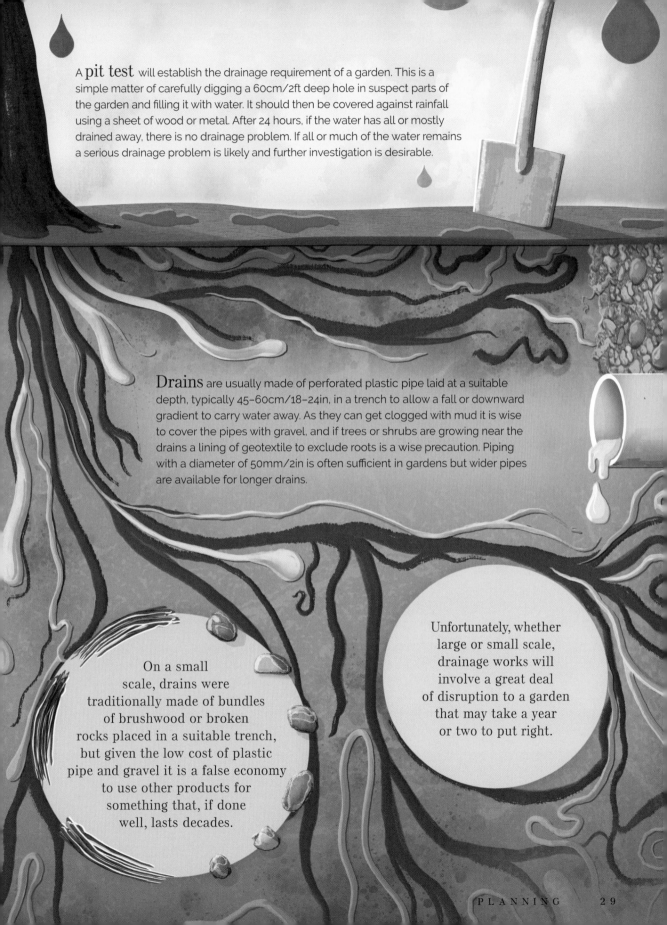

A **pit test** will establish the drainage requirement of a garden. This is a simple matter of carefully digging a 60cm/2ft deep hole in suspect parts of the garden and filling it with water. It should then be covered against rainfall using a sheet of wood or metal. After 24 hours, if the water has all or mostly drained away, there is no drainage problem. If all or much of the water remains a serious drainage problem is likely and further investigation is desirable.

**Drains** are usually made of perforated plastic pipe laid at a suitable depth, typically 45–60cm/18–24in, in a trench to allow a fall or downward gradient to carry water away. As they can get clogged with mud it is wise to cover the pipes with gravel, and if trees or shrubs are growing near the drains a lining of geotextile to exclude roots is a wise precaution. Piping with a diameter of 50mm/2in is often sufficient in gardens but wider pipes are available for longer drains.

On a small scale, drains were traditionally made of bundles of brushwood or broken rocks placed in a suitable trench, but given the low cost of plastic pipe and gravel it is a false economy to use other products for something that, if done well, lasts decades.

Unfortunately, whether large or small scale, drainage works will involve a great deal of disruption to a garden that may take a year or two to put right.

# Paths

Paths are useful but in a small garden they can take up valuable space, divide the garden awkwardly, spoil views and be costly to instal. It might be better to consider gravel or a similar covering that is practical and also offers planting possibilities.

Unfortunately **lawns are unable** to bear heavy footfall, and certainly not vehicles. Gravel is better at absorbing traffic, but only if it is laid on suitably firm underpinning. On clay or other wet soil, substantial quantities of ballast or broken rocks might be needed to support gravel.

There are **technical fixes** for these problems which can work well, such as plastic cell panels that hold gravel in place and spread loading onto the underlying soil. Similar plastic and also concrete grids are offered which allow lawn grasses to grow in the interstices of the grids, protecting the grass from being crushed but allowing it to root below and grow up into the light.

**Gravel, wood** or **bark chips** make a sound path in areas other than lawn, perhaps with an underlying layer of geotextile to prevent mud creeping into the path from below and pegged edging boards to make a neat edge. This should last a few years and can be made more permanent or not as required. Because they do not become slippery in wet weather such paths are especially useful in shady parts of the garden, under trees perhaps. They also do not require much excavation and so are safe for tree roots.

Chips and gravel are a nuisance in lawn areas and here stepping stones that will not become slippery in wet conditions are a good compromise.

It is certainly **not the case** that driveways or main paths must be cast from concrete, surfaced in concrete sets or pavers. Nor do lesser paths need to be made of such durable materials as concrete slabs and paving bricks. There are of course exceptions – the need for regular access to compost bins, summerhouses and garden sheds is usually best fulfilled by a durable, all-weather path. However, once laid, a path of this type cannot easily be moved, so great care should be taken in their installation.

They should be laid flush so the mower passes over them, and of even shape so that they can be quickly 'edged' to keep them smart.

Paths are **sometimes expanded** to become driveways or parking spaces. As this takes up much room and reduces possibilities for planting or relaxing, consider carefully before going ahead.

**Sometimes paths** can serve more than one function, which helps compensate for the cost and loss of garden space. Paths between lawn edges (flush with the turf for ease of mowing) and borders make a good permanent break, for example, and paths laid beside hedges allow access for trimming.

# Patio

Outdoor 'living' rooms require shelter from wind, a paved surface and a spot close to the house for entertaining. The patio serves this function and is often high on the list of any garden improvements. That no mowing or weeding is required is a major plus for many people, but on the other hand planting is constrained. The remedy is to use containers, raised beds or narrow strips of planting along the edges.

To some extent patio construction materials are dictated by aspect and air flow. Decking, a wonderfully quick and easy-to-construct surface, is less rewarding if not in the fullest sun as it can become covered in algae and slippery.

Gravel, unless a self-binding material is chosen, is not comfortable to walk on and is not an ideal surface for garden furniture or barbecues, both commonly considered essential parts of a well-functioning patio. A mixture of gravel and slabs is more practical, particularly in shady places where a patio might be slow to dry out after rain.

Bricks, concrete slabs or pavers form a cost-effective and durable surface, and can be chosen to match the house masonry. Robust construction with sufficient ballast or stones to support the patio area is required, and can be expensive. The closer to the house a patio is situated, the more practical and usable it will be. French doors link indoor and outdoor living areas and are a major advantage. A slight slope away from the house for good drainage is wise.

Sometimes the back of the house is not well positioned for good light and warmth. It may be north-facing, for example. In this case, it is worth placing the patio where it will catch the light, even if at a less than convenient distance from the house. Extending water and electricity to a more distant patio is a wise investment, as is a summerhouse to accommodate furniture and utensils. A well laid, sufficiently wide, and ideally illuminated path is also a good idea if best value is to be obtained from a patio.

In small gardens patios may take up a high proportion of available space and are often best if attractive in their own right. Using a mix of materials, such as slabs divided and edged with paving bricks, or alternating slabs with gravel or pebbles set in cement, are possibilities. Edging with vertical tiles or kerbing also adds interest. Making a patio too predictable and square tends to make it appear to be small – whereas using edges that are angled or merge into plantings helps to deceive the eye as to the patio's boundaries. Mirrors and *trompe l'oeil* can be used, with discretion, to playfully make a patio feel larger than it is.

# Greenhouse

Greenhouses are usually all about light, especially in winter. Exceptions might be ferneries, but in other cases a shaded greenhouse is very much inferior to one sited in an open location. Ideally there should be no other structures nor any large plants within 2m/6½ft, and indeed no tall trees or buildings to the south. The reality of modern gardens is that in most cases shade cannot be avoided, although it may be possible to reduce it to a minimum.

A greenhouse **without heating** limits what can be grown, but is still useful for summer vegetables and salad crops, and no heat is needed for alpines. Few people can afford to provide hothouse conditions (no less than 18°C/64°F), but keeping greenhouses frost-free is feasible in many cases and this permits the overwintering of popular plants such as citrus and standard argyranthemums, fuchsias and pelargoniums, which can be put outside from late spring until early autumn.

**Similarly**, a minimum of heating can allow apricots, peaches and grapes to flower early without the risk of frost damage that often curtails them outdoors. Lean-to greenhouses are ideal for this purpose.

A **greenhouse heated** in late winter can be used to raise young plants that need a long growing season, such as tender begonias, nicotiana, peppers, petunia and tomatoes.

W ←

Ideally there should be **ample vents** (windows) in the greenhouse roof. The equivalent to 20 per cent of the floor area is ideal but seldom achieved in low-cost greenhouses.

When that essential instrument, the minimum-maximum **thermometer,** indicates that high temperatures (greater than 30°C/86°F) are likely, it is advisable to shade with special white paint or netting draped over the outside.

Although gas and paraffin heaters are available, electric fan heaters are generally more practical.

E

**Orientating the greenhouse** so the long side runs east to west will allow in slightly more winter light, and is ideal for alpine houses or those used to grow plants over winter.

# Conservatory

Outdoor living is weather-dependent. A conservatory brings
the garden indoors in a way that houseplants do not quite manage.
But a conservatory forms part of the house, and the humid
atmosphere required by plants can be uncomfortable and limit
fittings and furnishing. Summer temperature control options are more
limited than for greenhouses, but these factors can be countered by
fitting wider doors. By having a nearby patio with lighting, the garden is
well set-up for outdoor living.

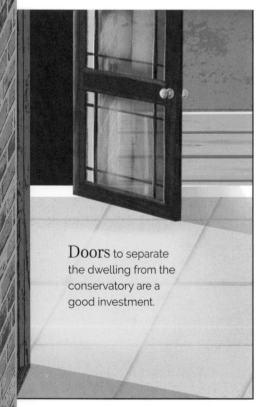

**Doors** to separate
the dwelling from the
conservatory are a
good investment.

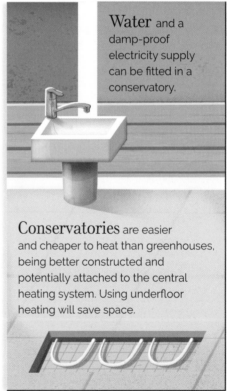

**Water** and a
damp-proof
electricity supply
can be fitted in a
conservatory.

**Conservatories** are easier
and cheaper to heat than greenhouses,
being better constructed and
potentially attached to the central
heating system. Using underfloor
heating will save space.

**Tiled floors** are better suited to plants than other
flooring, and for keen growers, drainage can be considered.

These structures are optimized for comfort rather than for light transmission, particularly if double glazed. **Ventilation** is often limited, as roof vents are omitted to avoid drips and draughts.

It is **less** costly, if not exactly cheap, to grow hothouse plants in the conservatory than in a greenhouse.

As for **aspect**, a south-facing conservatory tends to get too hot unless equipped with expensive shading, ideally as external blinds, while a north-facing aspect is dark enough to limit what plants can be grown.

'Indoor - outdoor' plants are an option, such as citrus, which stand out in summer and are brought indoors for the winter.

Some plants, such as grapes, need winter cold to crop well, and and in this case the conservatory is best unheated in winter.

As with greenhouses, size is important. Small sunrooms are much less suitable to plants than larger structures.

# Difficult sites

Gardens seldom have regular shapes, good drainage and fertile soil. If they do, growing plants is easy, but all too often conditions can be very discouraging. With sufficient funds any problematic site can be transformed into one without significant drawbacks, but in real life this is seldom the case. Happily, plants can grow in surprising places, and going with the flow by choosing tolerant subjects often gives satisfying, affordable results in a short time.

Gardens can become **wet** and **impassable** in winter, and **dry** and **dusty** in summer. For seasonally flooded gardens tolerant plants such as alders, dogwoods, iris, elders, poplars and willows make the bones of a satisfying garden.

It is unwise to fill in abandoned **ponds** and **swimming pools**, particularly if made of concrete, without making sure all hindrance to drainage is removed. If this is not possible and drainage remains questionable, it is sometimes possible to adjust the water level and put a little soil over the infill to make a bog garden full of the sorts of treasures that are so hard to accommodate in well-drained places: *Astilbe*, *Filipendula* and *Zantedeschia* for example.

**New builds** may have small gardens with damaged soils often laid over discarded building waste. Ways to deal with these problems include bringing in fresh soil, using paving instead of lawns, and enhancing the drainage and soil in any pits dug for tree-planting.

In very **acid** or **alkaline gardens**, it is often easy enough to add lime to remedy acid soils and either replace alkaline soil or acidify it by adding sulphur.

**Overgrown trees** can be expensive to remove and doing so also decreases privacy and opens views to unsightly vistas. Removing just the lower branches, however, improves access and opens lines of sight, letting in more light and avoiding costly tree surgery to reduce and limit crowns.

# Elements of design

Engaging a garden designer, even if only to advise on the potential and key aspects of the site, or perhaps do some drawings, is usually a very good investment. Very often however, people have their own ideas, or they may fancy trying their hand at designing their own plot, or perhaps part of it.

While it is wise to let a garden's design follow the intended function, there is no reason, other than perhaps cost and time, to rule anything out, no matter how fanciful. After all, a private garden is just that, a personal piece of space for the owners to use and enjoy as they see fit.

The choice of style can be overwhelming when planning a garden, what with colourful borders, long vistas, formal beds and romantic wild areas. It is impossible to do everything (unless you own a large estate). Instead, it is worth thinking about the essentials first: trees for height, boundaries, and what is already in the garden and worth keeping.

Gather information – spontaneity is good, but the cost and longevity of a garden design make planning worthwhile.

List what the garden needs to provide in order to fit in with the owner's lifestyle – play area, quiet retreat or outdoor entertaining?

Front garden views from house windows, and what you encounter when leaving the back or patio doors, are the areas of the garden you will enjoy most frequently.

Time available for upkeep – from low-maintenance to time-devouring, all-consuming hobby.

Sustainability can be planned into a garden design by re-using plants and by providing for wildlife.

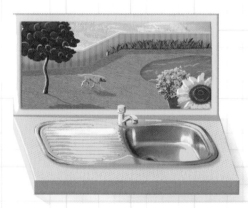

Plan an attractive view from the kitchen sink, if placed by a window, to make time spent doing chores more of a pleasure.

Broad and unbroken skylines can be incorporated into the long view from the garden, and features in the landscape can be framed with planting and structures.

Boldness in sweeping curves of borders, grass and paving avoids an overall 'bitty' look, which is seldom attractive and greatly increases the maintenance required.

Colour is a top priority and as such can be a source of anxiety. While a simple scheme of all, or almost all, one colour can work, a more satisfying approach is to consider colours that might clash (in a good and exciting way) or sit peacefully side by side without being dull.

# Gardens for children

Interest a child
in gardening and they can gain an
understanding of the natural world and their place in it,
plus of course a hobby, rich in health and happiness, for life.
A decline in interest in the teenage and young adult years often follows
but they will probably come back to it when they have a home,
and indeed children, of their own.

**Young minds** and fingers particularly appreciate the bright colours, flavours,
scents and textures of plant material. Slow-growing and subtle plants won't have as much
impact as the speedy and surprising ones.

**Creepy crawlies** are fascinating for the young. Bug hotels, plants that attract pollinators and butterflies, stones for slow-worms and newts to hide under and shallow water features can add to this interest (remember, though, that infants can drown in a few inches of water).

**Healthy eating** is reported to be more likely if children grow their own vegetables and fruit. Cherry tomatoes, pumpkins and strawberries are popular.

Children and **unusual foods** seldom mix, but edible flowers such as savoury hawthorn, sweet daylilies, peppery rocket and nasturtium flowers or pretty violets may interest a youthful palate.

**Colours** and associated dyes derived from flowers and other plant parts are an absorbing aspect of gardening that reaches into children's lives.

**Surface** and **sound** are also of interest to children. Think rattling nigella heads, coarse-grained sunflower seed heads, woolly stachys leaves, exploding seed pods of impatiens, and rustling grasses and bamboos.

**Visiting gardens** is often overlooked but they can be favourite places, especially overgrown wooded gardens or those with mazes of thickets or even formal mazes (although the borders may cause yawns).

**Fun things** like miniature gardens with small plants, flowers and moss lawns, or planting up a wheelbarrow can enthuse children.

# Planting

# Lawns

There is nothing quite like a lawn as an attractive and functional element of the garden, a place to entertain and for children to play. However, the reputation of lawns as being rather high maintenance and environmentally unsound is not unfounded, but much can be done to counter this.

**Lawns demand** less upkeep if there are no fiddly areas that take a long time to mow and edge. They are also easier to keep attractive if narrow paths that get excessively worn are avoided.

**Lawns** and **shade** do not go together and while shade-tolerant grasses are available, it is often better to choose different ground covering options, such as paving, or suitable perennials and shrubs.

Where **shade-tolerant** grass proves successful it requires slightly different maintenance than grass in full sun, by not mowing nearly as close to the soil as in the open. Shade lawns are typically less velvety than a fine sward and also less able to tolerate foot traffic.

Many lawns suffer from lack of initial preparation. It is worthwhile to spend time clearing debris, stones and weeds, loosening compacted areas with a fork and raking level, and treading to consolidate loose, dry (never wet) soil. Ideally this is done several months before laying turf or spreading grass seed to allow time for the soil to settle (level turf is hard to achieve if the soil settles unevenly) and weeds to be eradicated.

Wet gardens, perhaps where an impermeable clay soil is found, can benefit from turf being laid on an 8cm/3in layer of coarse sand. The grass roots thrive in the sand and explore the underlying clay for nutrients and moisture. The lack of sogginess means the lawn is more frequently usable.

Frequent mowing in the growing season, the use of lawn fertilizer in spring, and a weeding regime that usually is accomplished by lawn weedkillers, will keep a lawn looking good. Buying a mower that is sufficiently manoeuvrable and has as wide a cut as feasible for the garden will make mowing less irksome.

# Hedges

Hedges are an environmentally beneficial and potentially inexpensive way of enclosing plots, but have lost out as gardens have become smaller. They take up room to grow and need access to maintain. Some hedges need cutting twice a year or more, but the best hedges only need an annual trim, importantly ensuring the base is slightly wider than the top to avoid the loss of lower branches.

Traditionally, a background of **neutral mossy green** is favoured. All of these green hedges need trimming just once a year, in late summer: conifers such as Leyland cypress (× *Cuprocyparis leylandii* ) and yew (*Taxus baccata*); broad-leaved evergreens such as Portugal laurel (*Prunus lusitanica*) and holly (*Ilex aquifolium*); and deciduous beech (*Fagus sylvatica*) and hornbeam (*Carpinus betulus*). Both beech and hornbeam retain their russet leaves over winter.

However, coloured foliage such as *Photinia* 'Red Robin' and × *Cuprocyparis leylandii* 'Castlewellan', or variegated leaves such as the gold/green *Elaeagnus* × *ebbingei* 'Limelight' and *Ilex aquifolium* 'Handsworth New Silver', can also be used for hedging that is intended to provide colour in its own right.

Native deciduous trees, especially beech and hornbeam, are traditional hedging plants with especially good environmental properties, although not perhaps as 'smart' as formal hedges. Examples include: common spindle (*Euonymus europaeus*), hawthorn (*Crataegus monogyna*), guelder rose (*Viburnum opulus*), hazel (*Corylus avellana*), holly (*Ilex aquifolium*), field maple (*Acer campestre*) and oak (*Quercus robur* or *Quercus petraea*, which, like beech, retain their autumn leaves over winter). Blackthorn or sloe (*Prunus spinosa*) and elder (*Sambucus nigra*) are too invasive to be good garden hedges. Cherry plums (*Prunus cerasifera*) are also effective, including purple-leaved forms.

Suitable plants for **small** and **medium** hedges include:

Box-leaved holly
(*Ilex crenata*)

Semi-evergreen shrubby
honeysuckle
(*Lonicera nitida*)

Narrow-leaved mock privet
(*Phillyrea angustifolia*)

Yew
(*Taxus baccata*)

**Broad-leaved** evergreens are the commonest **garden hedging** plants:

Privet
(*Ligustrum ovalifolium*)

Golden privet
(*Ligustrum ovalifolium*
'Aureum')

Holm oak
(*Quercus ilex*)

Cherry laurel
(*Prunus laurocerasus*)

Portugal laurel
(*Prunus lusitanica*)

Thorny berberis
(*Berberis julianae*)

Pyracantha

Deciduous berberis

# Screens

Hedges are not the only planting method for shelter and privacy, and other options have become more feasible and affordable with the wider production and sale of semi-mature plants. By using taller trees and other structures, overviews from neighbouring properties can be reduced and unsightly objects outside the garden can be made less conspicuous.

Traditionally, large gardens in exposed situations have belts of trees planted to intercept winds, typically alders (*Alnus* species), beech (*Fagus* species), pines (*Pinus* species) and poplar (*Populus* species) planted to intercept the prevailing winds. Adding a further belt of shrubs improves protection by reducing air flow through the trunks. Few gardens have the space for this, but the principle is the same – choosing taller plants that filter the wind.

For the scale of most gardens, hedges are a more practical option, but a mixed planting of deciduous and evergreen shrubs provide a garden feature as well as keeping off the prevailing wind.

**Evergreen trees** have a year-round effect but except for conifers, relatively few are offered; eucalyptus and holm oak are the best choices for windbreaks. Conifers, including Lawson's cypress (*Chamaecyparis lawsoniana*), Leyland cypress (*Cupressus × leylandii*) and western red cedar (*Thuja plicata*) are common choices, being fast-growing, but they do not respond well to pruning in situations where they need to be kept small. **Deciduous trees** are usually the best option despite their winter bareness, particularly birches (*Betula* species) or mountain ash (*Sorbus aucuparia*).

**Taller trees** cast shade and where this needs to be limited the options include growing species that respond well to pruning, or considering multi-stemmed trees that have been trained from early life into highly picturesque forms with several trunks, where width comes at the expense of height. Fastigiate or narrow trees (*Quercus robur* 'Fastigiata' or *Carpinus betulus* 'Fastigiata', for example) also limit shade.

**Ready trained**, including pleached, **trees** are widely offered for instant effect. These include field maple, hornbeam, beech, holly, pear, oak and limes, especially the red-twigged *Tilia platyphyllos* 'Rubra'.

# Dry and sunny planting

Sunny areas of the garden, particularly where the soil is sandy, and sites located in low-rainfall regions lend themselves to 'dry gardens' planted with sun-lovers that need no watering in summer, but are hardy enough to survive winter. However, they will seldom tolerate waterlogging so good drainage is also required.

**Mediterranean** plants including lavender, rosemary and Jerusalem sage are reasonably hardy and able to survive the driest summers.

Grey, resinous, waxy or woolly leaves, usually small and narrow or spiky, are signs of **drought-resistance**. Plants suited to dry locations often have compact, low-growing habits.

Herbaceous plants for **dry sunny places** include acanthus, cardoons (*Cynara cardunculus*), echinops, evening primroses (*Oenothera* species), fennel (*Foeniculum vulgare*), *Stachys byzantina* and *Verbascum olympicum*.

Trees should **cast little shade** and be used with caution – there is just not enough sunlight in mild climates to penetrate tree shade. However, shrubs can work well. Mount Etna broom (*Genista aetnensis*) and the pineapple broom (*Argyrocytisus battandieri*) make large shrub-trees that relish dry, sunny sites.

Among the **smaller shrubs** for dry planting, brooms (*Cytisus* such as low-growing yellow-flowered (*C. lydia*) and *Cistus* are good choices,

**Sub-shrubs** are the mainstay of dry gardens. These plants have a woody base but produce new herbaceous growth each year. Examples include silvery *Artemisia* and *Helichrysum italicum*, as well as grey-green *Ballota pseudodictamnus* and *Euphorbia characias* subsp. *wulfenii*.

Some **grasses** are suitable too: blue oat grass (*Helictotrichon sempervirens*), Korean feather reed grass (*Calamagrostis brachytricha*) and Giant feather grass (*Stipa gigantea*).

Another useful **characteristic** of plants adapted to regions with fierce hot, dry summers is that many take shelter below ground. These bulbs include alliums, eremurus, hardy cyclamen and species tulips. Gardeners can use these creatively to add drama in spring (tulips), early summer (alliums) or winter (cyclamen).

Although drainage should be good, fertility should be poor as leafy succulent shoots are susceptible to disease and frost damage. Also, excess leaves are produced at the expense of flowers.

# Shade planting

Shade, particularly dry shade under trees, can present a planting challenge, especially when a high proportion of a small garden is shaded. On the other hand, a garden without shade is less pleasant in high summer than one with at least some soothing shade.

**Hardy geraniums** have very attractive foliage but also flower well in early summer, and after shearing off provide fresh late summer foliage; black widow (*Geranium phaeum*) and cultivars, with abundant small dainty dark recurved flowers, are very shade tolerant,

**Hostas** or plantain **lilies**, if slugs and snails can be repelled, are the most striking of shade plants.

Smaller, **thicker-leaved hostas** seem less attractive to slugs and suit all shady borders. *Hosta* 'Blue Mouse Ears' is a small, mounded, blue-leaved example.

For **deep shade**, *Astrantia maxima* offers pink summer flowers, epimediums have spring flowers, and pulmonarias produce white, blue or pink flowers in spring.

For **lighter shade**, lady's mantle (*Alchemilla mollis*) has striking light green foliage at its best when wet from rain or dew. Many heucheras have unusual foliage, including *Heuchera* 'Plum Pudding', with red leaves, and yellow 'Lime Marmalade'. Bleeding hearts such as *Dicentra formosa* 'Bacchanal' have nodding red flowers in spring and summer, while for white-and-pink flowers opt for *Lamprocapnos spectabilis*.

Big, bold yellow-green *Hosta* 'Sum and Substance' is a magnificent plant for moist shade.

**Evergreen shrubs** suit deeper shade well, especially under deciduous trees. Butcher's broom (*Ruscus aculeatus*), mahonias, evergreen berberis and viburnums are among this group. **Lime-hating** (ericaceous) camellia, rhododendron and pieris are excellent shade-lovers but unless the soil is acid are best grown in containers of ericaceous potting media, when they make very rewarding plants for a shaded patio.

# Water planting

Water plants need **water** and **soil** of the right quality, lack of flow, suitable water depth and more or less constant water levels, and, crucially, little or no shade. Seasonal ponds that dry out in summer are hard to plant as few species tolerate alternating dry conditions and immersion.

You should provide **water depths** of 25–60cm/10–24in, and erring on the deep side is best when constructing ponds, as the deeper water provides a favourable surface-to-volume ratio that minimises temperature and other fluctuations. Very small or containerised ponds are often stressful for plants, although they can be valuable to wildlife, or as a patio feature. Plants requiring shallow water can be planted on ledges, bricks or even crates.

Water lilies are the best of the deep-water plants, requiring 20–60cm/ 8–24in of water, but are usually planted shallowly at first, then gradually lowered to their final depth.

Unlike most water lilies, the diminutive white-flowered *Nymphaea* 'Pygmaea Helvola' needs hardly any water at all and is one of the best for container ponds or other shallow situations.

**White water lilies**, such as *Nymphaea* 'Gonnère', are especially attractive. For pink and red, *N.* 'Masaniello' and *N.* 'Escarboucle' are outstanding. Other colours include yellow *N.* 'Marliacea Chromatella'.

Other plants for **deeper water** include golden club (*Orontium aquaticum*), with yellow flower spikes over its floating foliage, and water hawthorn (*Aponogeton distachyos*), which has shapely oval leaves and small, fragrant white flowers.

Many **floating plants** are too tender to plant in outdoor pools, including water lettuce (*Pistia* species), sold by aquarist suppliers. However, the spiky white-flowered water soldier (*Stratiotes aloides*) and frogbit (*Hydrocharis morsus-ranae*), with round leaves and yellow-centred white summer flowers, are both hardy.

**Submerged plants** are good for pond health. Try water crowfoot (*Ranunculus aquatilis*) with elegant, small cup-shaped flowers on stalks gracefully held above the water, or water violet (*Hottonia palustris*) with feathery foliage and plumes of white, yellow-centred flowers.

# Container planting

Gardeners use containers to grow plants in places where there is no soil, including indoors, and for giving plants the conditions they need whatever the garden soil may be like. They also offer the option to move plants under cover during winter, or shift them around the garden to where they can be used to best effect.

Containers can be objects of **beauty**, but any baskets, boxes, pots, sacks or bags, tubs or stacks of tyres may be used, as long as soil is retained and water can drain away.

Soil for pots is very different to native garden soil. It has to hold moisture and nutrients in small volumes of material, yet provide support and good drainage. Soils for this purpose are called potting composts or potting media. 'Media' is better, as potting soils are not composted, but compounded from bark chips, wood fibre, coir (coconut husk), grit, expanded minerals such as perlite and vermiculite, sand and, controversially, peat. Lime and fertilizer are added to adjust the chemical environment of the roots. Air-filled spaces are crucial – potting media full of air spaces may seem expensive, but too little air leads to 'drowned' roots, especially if the medium is wet. Potting media break down over time, losing air spaces and leading to injured plants. Therefore long-term planting, trees and shrubs for example, needs compost with plenty of air space. Even so, it is advisable to repot every three years in late winter before growth begins.

Any plant can be induced to grow in containers, but particularly good choices include:

## Climbers:
Akebia, clematis and solanum. Lanky climbers act as a giant 'wick', so a large tub with a diameter of at least 60cm/2ft is advisable.

## Annuals and bedding:
Nasturtiums, pelargoniums, petunias and, for shade, begonias and fuchsias.

## Vegetables:
Aubergines, peppers (including chilli), tomatoes and baby salad leaves. Also herbs – for shade mint, and chives.

## Perennials:
*Dianthus* (pinks), geraniums, hostas and sedum.

Among the grasses, *Festuca glauca*, graceful *Hakonechloa macra* and *Luzula sylvatica* 'Aurea' (a yellow-leaved sedge). For bamboo, ruscus-leaved *Shibataea kumasaca*.

## Shrubs:
For shade, camellia and rhododendron (in acidic potting media), fatsia and skimmia (in ordinary potting media). Choisya for sun.

## Trees:
Birches and maples (including Japanese maples). Pots slightly stunt trees in a good way, keeping them smaller and picturesque.

# Wildflowers

Native wildflowers are worth growing for their simple beauty, as well as their benefit to wildlife. There are essentially two kinds of **true wildflower** for gardens: cornfield annuals and meadow plants. The former are annuals whose lifecycle mimics the cereal fields in which they thrived before the use of agricultural herbicides. The latter are mainly perennials that grow in grassy areas, usually with good sun, although there are woodland wildflowers as well. Seed is available as mixtures formulated for particular soils and conditions – sunny, dry, limestone areas or shady clay meadows, for example. Mixtures are highly convenient, but there is no reason why gardeners cannot create their own mixtures, as the individual species are also available, and inexpensive.

'Wildflowers' can also be slightly misapplied to plants that may have been **bred from wildflowers**, such as garden cornflowers and Shirley poppies bred from their cornfield counterparts, or similar species such as California poppy *(Eschscholzia californica)* and *Clarkia*. European perennial 'meadows' contain such non-native plants as the Asian yarrow cultivar, *Achillea filipendulina* 'Cloth of Gold' and the North American yellow coneflower, *Rudbeckia fulgida* var. *deamii*, which belongs to the daisy family. These 'almost-wild' flowers are very colourful and are highly beneficial to insects and other wildlife.

**When growing** true wildflowers, best practice is to use locally collected seeds. County wildlife trusts can usually advise on where to get suitable seeds. Some wildflower seed on sale is actually grown abroad. Widespread use of such seed could dilute the genes associated with plants adapted to local conditions and cause long-term harm. Another problem is that seed raised in cultivation gradually 'drifts' from the characteristics that made it successful in the wild to being a plant that succeeds in cultivation. Good suppliers refresh their stock from legally and sustainably harvested wild seed every six years or so.

Neither **cornfield annuals** nor **meadow plants** benefit from rich, fertile soils, as annual weeds can overcome cornfield flowers and grasses become rampant when the soil is rich. Reducing fertility can be challenging, particularly with clay soils that naturally have a very high background level of plant nutrients. On a small scale, the turf or topsoil can be removed and wildflower seed sown into the the remaining subsoil.

Another **relatively easy** method is to cover the original soil with 8cm/3in of coarse sand and sow into this weed-free and infertile medium. The wildflowers will root into the underlying soil for water and nutrients. Grass seed should be used sparingly and cautiously, as removing over-vigorous grasses is very difficult. Yellow rattle (*Rhinanthus minor*), a native wildflower, parasitizes grasses and can take some of the steam out of them, allowing other wildflowers to thrive.

# Bee-friendly planting

Bees are valuable pollinators, without which many plants could not set seed and some crops (apples, strawberries and tomatoes, for example) would be unproductive. They are also large, as insects go, easy to recognize, and often attractive. Sadly, their numbers have fallen with changes in farm practice, loss of countryside to development and, in the case of honeybees, new ailments.

As well as honeybees, kept in hives for their honey or living wild in nests in hollow trees or gaps in brickwork, there are bumblebees that make small nests and solitary bees that typically live in tunnels in soil, walls and timber. Solitary bees are often overlooked, being small and making no nests, but they too are highly effective pollinators.

Gardens are amazingly fruitful places for bees. Indeed, one authority maintains that every other garden harbours a bumblebee nest. Honeybees gather nectar and pollen for more than 3 kilometres/2 miles around their hive.

Bees need nectar as 'aviation fuel' and many bees, including honeybees, feed their young on pollen.

Bees come out of their over-wintering state in early spring and begin to forage for food. This is a critical time – to maintain their numbers they need to build up their breeding population fast to take advantage of the flush of flowers in early summer. Willows flower early and although wind-pollinated produce highly nutritious pollen. Woolly willow (*Salix lanata*, male form) and halberd willow (*Salix hastata* 'Wehrhahnii'), are good garden willows.

# PLANTING SUGGESTIONS
## TO MAKE YOUR PLOT BEE PRODUCTIVE

In **spring** flowering trees and shrubs are heavily used by bees: flowering cherries, berberis and flowering and fruiting currants, including redcurrants, are good choices. Evergreens are harder to source, but pieris (acid soils only), skimmia and cherry laurel are productive for bees.

By early **summer**, flowers are abundant: garden plants such as lavender (*Lavandula*), mullein (*Verbascum*) and Japanese spirea (*Spiraea japonica*) complement the many native flowers blooming at this time. Garden plants really come into their own in late summer, when they flower continuously at a time when native plants have finished flowering: honeywort (*Cerinthe major* 'Purpurascens') and red valerian (*Centranthus ruber*) are popular with bees.

**Autumn,** like spring, is crucial time, as the longer the bees can keep multiplying the better their chances of surviving the winter. Common ivy flowers deep into autumn and is always awash with bees. Dahlias (single-flowered ones) and Chinese and Japanese anemones (*Anemone hupehensis /A. × hybrida*) are highly ornamental and feed bees late in the season.

Even in **winter** bees may need to forage on sunny days; crocus, snowdrops (*Galanthus nivalis*), hellebores and shrubby honeysuckles (*Lonicera × purpusii*) are reliable flowering plants that are easy to fit into even small gardens.

# Mixed borders

Mixed borders have long been the staple of gardens, with herbaceous flowers, spring and summer bulbs, roses, well-chosen shrubs, small climbers and foliage plants meshing together to form a relatively stable and persistent planting with a long season of interest. If there is enough space, mixed borders for particular shorter seasons are also feasible – early summer borders can be based on irises, lupins and peonies, with flowering shrubs such as choisya and mock orange (*Philadelphus*) for example. Borders typically flow beside paths, or paths curve through them.

Colour is a fraught matter, hence the popularity of white gardens. But beds usually look well in similar colours, from pink, say, through violet and purple to red, with contrasting flashes of orange and softening whites and greens. In truth, many borders are periodically 'edited' by replacing plants until the desired effect is achieved. Colour, however, is not the only aspect to require arrangement. Leaf shapes to contrast and coordinate are an opportunity for subtle beauty. Similarly, variations in height add interest to a border.

Herbaceous plants are the mainstay, with early summer colour coming from purple allium heads, astrantia, aquilegias, foxgloves, hardy geraniums, rodgersias, with large corrugated leaves and frothy pink flowers, and verbascums. Later summer interest is provided by achillea, crocosmia, daylilies (*Hemerocallis*), rudbeckia, penstemon, salvia and sedum. A final flourish in September comes from such plants as *Hesperantha coccinea* and Japanese anemones. Smaller plants are conventionally used for the front of the border, such as lady's mantle (*Alchemilla mollis*), London pride (*Saxifraga × urbium*) or the blue-green grass *Festuca glauca*. Another approach is to use slender, taller plants such as *Verbena bonariensis* to make a kind of floral mist in front of the border for romantic effect.

**Certain situations** complicate life – dry soils, for example. Grey-leaved artemisia and stachys are water-saving, as are verbascums, spiky red-hot pokers (*Kniphofia*) and succulent sedums. Ornamental grasses, too, are drought-tolerant. Lavender, phlomis (shrubby and herbaceous) and rosemary are also sound.

**Shade** also limits the choice of plants. Mixed borders are in fact unwise in partial shade. The yellow *Luzula sylvatica* 'Aurea' and sedges such as *Carex oshimensis* 'Evergold' (variegated yellow) are notably resilient. Other shade-tolerant subjects include elephant ears (*Bergenia*), hardy geraniums, hostas, *Epimedium, Liriope muscari* and periwinkle (*Vinca*).

Although ideally plants look best grouped in threes, fives or sevens, in small beds ones or twos are often necessary. Here, a single plant will provide a strong presence and 'carry' the bed. Try *Hibiscus syriacus*, Japanese maples, standard wisteria or roses, or, for added drama, the hardy Chinese windmill palm (*Trachycarpus fortunei*).

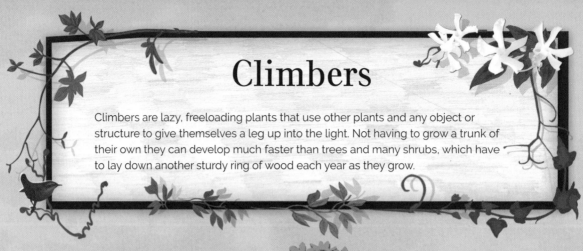

# Climbers

Climbers are lazy, freeloading plants that use other plants and any object or structure to give themselves a leg up into the light. Not having to grow a trunk of their own they can develop much faster than trees and many shrubs, which have to lay down another sturdy ring of wood each year as they grow.

Happily **man-made** environments are rich in suitable structures. Indeed, climbers should be encouraged in urban settings as they clothe buildings, keeping heat in during winter both by making an insulating blanket and by slowing air speed over structures, which minimizes cooling. In summer the opposite is the case: climbers keep off excess sun and by transpiring water have a cooling effect. They are easy on the eye compared to most masonry, too. Insects and birds find cover, breeding sites and food sources in bushy climbers. Unfortunately, climbers can also get into spots where they are unwelcome – gutters or roof voids, or between fence timbers or across windows – so annual maintenance is a requirement.

Climbers such as wisteria and roses can twine. Some, including clematis, cling using tendrils, while others use roots, hairs or suckers to bind to supports. Ivies (*Hedera* species), Virginia creeper (*Parthenocissus quinquefolia*) and climbing hydrangea (*Hydrangea anomala* subsp. *petiolaris*) are notable 'clingers'. Although clinging climbers need no wires or trellis to support them as do twining and tendril-equipped climbers, they can harm underlying masonry if the mortar is unsound; and when they need to be removed their suckers do not tear cleanly away, leaving unsightly fragments that are hard to detach from walls.

**Within gardens**, opportunities for climbers abound, as they can cover fences, sheds and walls. If these are insufficient, arbours, arches, pergolas, pillars, tripods, tunnels and wigwams can be constructed in strategic spots to enhance a view or blot out an eyesore. More climbers could be grown up trees. An big old unfruitful apple tree can readily support a vigorous climbing rose such as *Rosa filipes* 'Kiftsgate', for example.

Strictly speaking, climbers are actually ‘**climbing shrubs**’ except for some very useful annual and herbaceous ones, such as Spanish flag (*Ipomoea lobata*), glory flower (*Eccremocarpus scaber*) or everlasting sweet pea (*Lathyrus latifolius*). Many shrubs will adopt a sprawling or climbing habit if they encounter a suitable structure: glory pea (*Clianthus puniceus*), winter jasmine (*Jasminium nudiflorum*) and many roses, including the Modern English cultivars, are examples.

**Wisteria**, arguably the best climber, is ideally suited to south-facing aspects and indeed to west-facing ones. Climbing roses and clematis all thrive on south- and west-facing supports, but two slightly tender species, *Clematis armandii* and its cultivars and the yellow Banksian rose (*Rosa banksiae* 'Lutea'), are especially well suited if there is sufficient space and height.

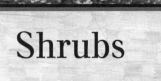

# Shrubs

Shrubs with a fine natural form, ideal for lawn or border specimens, include *Viburnum plicatum* f. *tomentosum* 'Mariesii', which flowers in early summer on 'layer cake' tiered branches. As it is spoilt by pruning, and ultimately needs about 2.5m/8¼ft to grow, it is one for open spaces, perhaps on lawns.

Shrubs are commonly **horribly mistreated**, being planted too densely, so that they make unsightly, forbidding thickets, which are then sheared each year to a blob or allowed to become overbearing through lack of pruning. Planting in excessive shade or sun leads to unhappy, stressed specimens. Yet, if given freedom to express their natural form, they make fine features for fences, lawns, mixed borders, walls and under trees. The trick is to identify their habit and requirements in advance.

For growing against **sunny walls** or **fences**, wall shrubs tend to be more robust and easier to manage than true climbers. Abutilons such as *Abutilon megapotamicum,* with curious red and yellow flowers, relish sunny walls and bloom for most of the year. Californian lilacs such as *Ceanothus* 'Italian Skies', with blue, late-spring flowers and small glossy leaves, are ideal, while for low walls under windows perhaps *Ceanothus* 'Blue Mound', which attains only 1.5m/5ft.

For evergreen specimens, *Osmanthus* × *burkwoodii* has scented tubular spring flowers and neat, small leaves much like box, but is more graceful.

**Under trees**, evergreen shrubs are a very useful form of ground cover. Mahonias such as the tall *Mahonia* × *media* 'Lionel Fortescue' are architectural and very usefully flower in the autumn. At the opposite end of the scale, the low-growing *Pachysandra terminalis* makes a neat and interesting ground cover.

Shrubs do **berries** well. *Clerodendrum trichotomum* var. *fargesii* has startling blue berries after fragrant white flowers, while *Callicarpa bodinieri* var. *giraldii* 'Profusion' carries bunches of little violet berries after small lilac flowers. Callicarpa produces berries most reliably if several plants can be grown to cross-pollinate each other. The yellow-fruited form of the guelder rose (*Viburnum opulus* 'Xanthocarpum'), with bright berries and coloured foliage before leaf fall in autumn, is especially choice.

**In spring**, after winter bulbs, snowdrops and daffodils, early-flowering shrubs are invaluable until the roses come in at midsummer. Spiraea × *cinerea* 'Grefsheim' starts off the display in many gardens, followed by the mock oranges (*Philadelphus*) with the evergreen *Choisya ternata*, both fragrant. Bright yellow is welcome in spring and is provided by forsythia and by bachelor's buttons (*Kerria japonica* 'Pleniflora').

# Trees

Trees are the ultimate form of vegetation – any terrain where there is enough rainfall and the climate is not too arctic or alpine will in its natural state carry forests. Trees grow big and often fast to overwhelm lesser plants. They can overwhelm gardeners, too, unless care is taken to match tree with site.

**Forest trees** are usually very large and fast-growing. Ash (*Fraxinus excelsior*), Douglas fir (*Pseudotsuga menziesii*), hybrid larch (*Larix × marschlinsii*), oaks (*Quercus*) and Scots pine (*Pinus sylvestris*) are examples, all of which should be allowed into gardens only with great caution. Children sometimes raise these from collected acorns and other fruits, and even though the resulting trees soon become large they are often retained, in a ragged condition, for sentimental reasons. The same goes for Christmas trees, which are in fact seedling forest trees. Curiously, many forest trees make excellent hedges: beech (*Fagus sylvatica*), hornbeam (*Carpinus betulus*) and Leyland cypress (× *Cuprocyparis leylandii*), for example.

**Less overbearing trees** can be used in streets. London plane (*Platanus × hispanica*) and lime (*Tilia cordata*, a species less prone to honeydew) are common for this purpose. Street trees are often heavily pruned from time to time, which does them no harm and makes them better neighbours.

Beech

Ash

Scots pine

Leyland cypress

Quercus robur

Lime

Hornbeams

London plane

Oak

Douglas fir

Leyland cypress

Hybrid larch

*Eucalyptus*

*Quercus*

*Sorbus*

*Prunus × schmittii*

*Eucryphia*

*Holm oak*

*Carpinus betulus*

*Pyrus*

*Arbutus unedo*

*Prunus pendula*

*Holly*

*Prunus*

*Douglas fir*

*Malus*

Evergreen trees (except conifers) are rather uncommon, which perhaps is as well since they cast a very deep shade and can be dank and drippy in winter. Some to consider include: eucalyptus, *Eucryphia × nymansensis* 'Nymansay', holm oak (*Quercus ilex*), common holly (*Ilex aquifolium*) and strawberry tree (*Arbutus unedo*).

Narrow or fastigiate trees are very good choices for adding a welcome upright in a garden where spread would be. These include *Carpinus betulus* 'Fastigiata', narrow flowering cherries *Prunus* 'Amanogawa' and *Prunus × schmittii*, and narrow mountain ash *Sorbus aucuparia* 'Joseph Rock'.

Weeping trees are often space-efficient, although one key advantage of a tree over shrubs is that it can be walked beneath, which is not always possible with weepers. Good weeping trees include the weeping crab apple *Malus* 'Royal Beauty', pink weeping cherry *Prunus pendula* 'Pendula Rubra', and the silvery weeping pear *Pyrus salicifolia* 'Pendula'.

Spring-flowering trees are prized in streets and gardens, but adding more cherries (*Prunus*) and crab apples (*Malus*) in particular is not necessarily the best use of limited space, as views of nearby flowering trees can be 'borrowed'. If neighbours have cherries and crab apples, for example, gardeners may wish to add early-flowering amelanchiers, ornamental pears (*Pyrus*) and magnolias, or fill in with later-flowering *Sorbus* (of the mountain ash family), yellow-flowered laburnums or flowering hawthorns (*Crataegus*) to complement the existing trees.

# Conifers

Conifers are covered with needle-like leaves and reproduce
by wind-pollinated cones, from which winged seeds are released.
These trees are a clever adaptation to short growing seasons or drought-prone
regions. Broad-leaved trees are most efficient in the summer, but evergreen
broad-leaved trees are vulnerable in the winter to weather damage and browsing by
herbivorous animals. This is why holly, for example, has extremely durable leaves
heavily armoured with spines. Deciduous trees avoid winter by shedding their leaves
and growing a new set in spring. This is costly in resources and takes time which, in
regions with a short growing season, puts them at a disadvantage to evergreen trees.

Conifer needles **are well adapted** to survive winter unscathed. Snow just
slides off rather than breaking branches (mature cedars are an exception). Some
conifers are deciduous of course, larch (*Larix*) for example, which grows in
alpine regions with fairly long, hot growing seasons but harsh winters.
Needles also shed heat and retain water, so Mediterranean pines and
cedars sweat out summer and do their growing in winter.

**Taller conifers** are rather brooding and they are seldom welcome in gardens, although make fine specimens in parks. Monkey puzzle (*Araucaria araucana*), blue cedar (*Cedrus atlantica* 'Glauca') and Christmas trees, usually Norway spruce (*Picea abies*) or Caucasian fir (*Abies nordmanniana*), are often unwisely planted in gardens, soon becoming much too big to remain.

**Many conifers** are offered as **dwarf**, which can really mean dwarf (*Chamaecyparis lawsoniana* 'Minima Aurea' attains 30cm/1ft after ten years) or very slow-growing, taking 10 years to reach 1m/3¼ft in the case of *Chamaecyparis pisifera* 'Boulevard', an old and very popular dwarf conifer capable of eventually reaching 10m/33ft .

**Dwarf trees** are effectively shrubs and can make striking specimens for borders. *Pinus mugo* is dumpy and an excellent miniature pine, ideally planted alone so its roundness can be appreciated. Column-like trees are common and include the juniper *Juniperus communis* 'Compressa', reaching 1m/3¼ft or less at maturity, the pyramidal *J. chinensis* 'Pyramidalis', up to 1.5m/5ft after 10 years, and *J. scopulorum* 'Skyrocket', attaining a very slender 1.8m/6ft after 10 years.

# Semi-mature plants

**Now that** semi-mature trees and other plants are more affordable, they are being used more widely. However, this is not a new technique. Lancelot 'Capability' Brown (who died on 6 February 1783) installed large mature trees in his famous 18th-century landscapes by the alarming method of cutting their roots (tree roots are mostly in the top 1m/3¼ft of the soil) and pulling the tree down with a team of horses, then dragging the unfortunate tree by horse power to a pre-prepared pit, planting it and then propping it up.

The development of **powered machinery** enabled a more sophisticated version of this process, during the building of the 'new towns' in the 1960s. These mechanical tree spades could scoop up a mature tree and much of its rootball at one gulp, to deposit it in a suitable planting pit. The same machines are still used today to shift inappropriately placed trees.

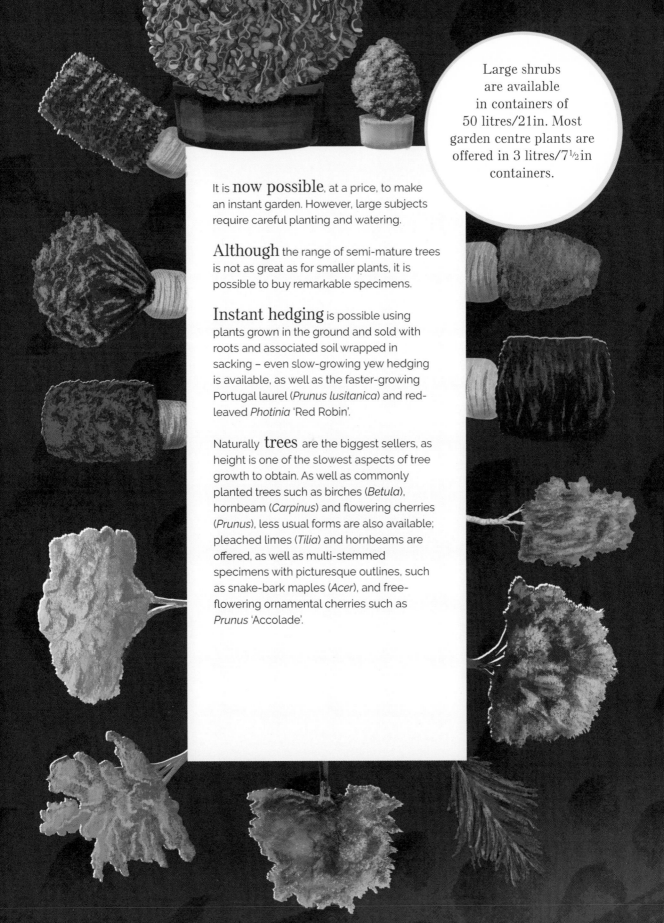

It is **now possible**, at a price, to make an instant garden. However, large subjects require careful planting and watering.

**Although** the range of semi-mature trees is not as great as for smaller plants, it is possible to buy remarkable specimens.

**Instant hedging** is possible using plants grown in the ground and sold with roots and associated soil wrapped in sacking – even slow-growing yew hedging is available, as well as the faster-growing Portugal laurel (*Prunus lusitanica*) and red-leaved *Photinia* 'Red Robin'.

Naturally **trees** are the biggest sellers, as height is one of the slowest aspects of tree growth to obtain. As well as commonly planted trees such as birches (*Betula*), hornbeam (*Carpinus*) and flowering cherries (*Prunus*), less usual forms are also available; pleached limes (*Tilia*) and hornbeams are offered, as well as multi-stemmed specimens with picturesque outlines, such as snake-bark maples (*Acer*), and free-flowering ornamental cherries such as *Prunus* 'Accolade'.

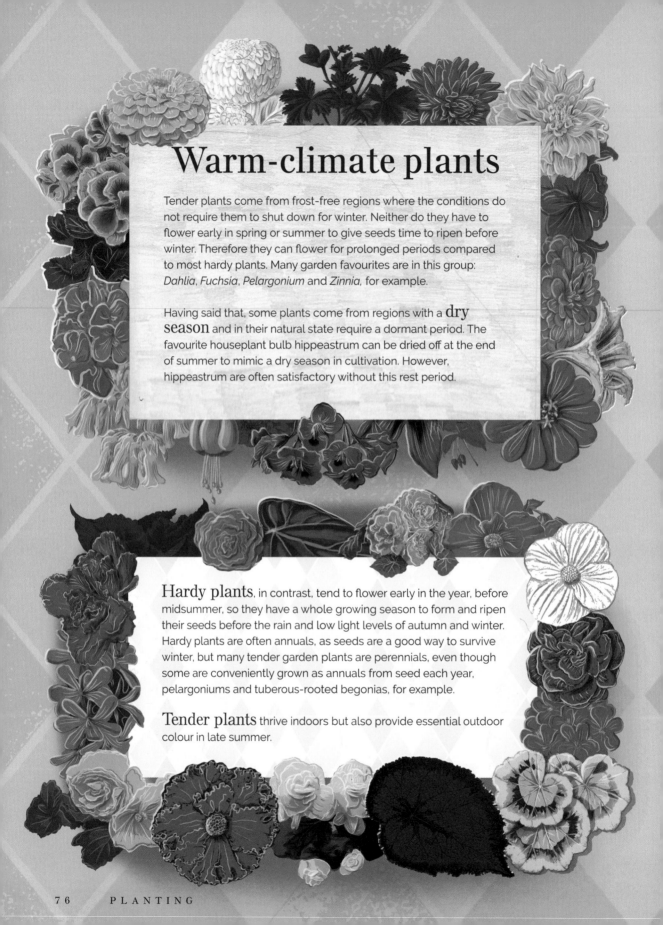

# Warm-climate plants

Tender plants come from frost-free regions where the conditions do not require them to shut down for winter. Neither do they have to flower early in spring or summer to give seeds time to ripen before winter. Therefore they can flower for prolonged periods compared to most hardy plants. Many garden favourites are in this group: *Dahlia*, *Fuchsia*, *Pelargonium* and *Zinnia*, for example.

Having said that, some plants come from regions with a **dry season** and in their natural state require a dormant period. The favourite houseplant bulb hippeastrum can be dried off at the end of summer to mimic a dry season in cultivation. However, hippeastrum are often satisfactory without this rest period.

**Hardy plants**, in contrast, tend to flower early in the year, before midsummer, so they have a whole growing season to form and ripen their seeds before the rain and low light levels of autumn and winter. Hardy plants are often annuals, as seeds are a good way to survive winter, but many tender garden plants are perennials, even though some are conveniently grown as annuals from seed each year, pelargoniums and tuberous-rooted begonias, for example.

**Tender plants** thrive indoors but also provide essential outdoor colour in late summer.

**Seed-raised** tender plants need a flying start, as by the time it is warm enough for them to grow outdoors from seed in late spring or early summer there is insufficient time for them to flower well before the winter frosts. This is particularly true in northern regions, where the growing season (period between last and first frosts) is short. Therefore seed is sown in heated greenhouses from mid-winter until late spring, starting with small seeds such as begonia and finishing with larger seeds such as nasturtium, which form big, vigorous seedlings that are soon ready to be planted outdoors. Plants are large and robust enough to plant outdoors from late spring to early summer after a two-week period of gradual acclimatization to cooler conditions called 'hardening off'.

In **dry spots**, and especially for hanging baskets and windowboxes, which are by nature very well drained and have limited root space, consider plants with some drought-tolerance such as *Lotus berthelotii* from the Canary Islands, the Australian *Scaevola* and the trailing pelargoniums from South Africa.

For **summer containers**, as well as bright, long-flowering *Nicotiana*, petunias and salvias, include foliage plants such as *Helichrysum* and *Coleus*. These suit sunny spots. But for foliage in shade, the green or variegated *Chlorophytum*, also familiar as a houseplant, is a good choice.

**Flowers** for shaded areas are more limited; fibrous-rooted begonias, impatiens and fuchsias are the most reliable.

# Choosing

# Annuals

Annuals grow and flower in one season, while the very similar biennials grow in the first season and flower in the next. They are fleeting and insubstantial, but also easy, cheap, fun and colourful. Many people get started on gardening with a packet of annuals.

Annuals may be hardy or tender. The latter need at least 12°C/54°F to thrive and are slain by frost. They are started off in a greenhouse or similar heated environment at 15–23°C/59–73°F, to be planted out after the last frosts. Tender annuals are raised in the same way as peppers and tomatoes.

Many so-called tender annuals are in fact perennials in hot climates, including *Begonia*, *Calibrachoa* and *Lobelia*, but are grown as annuals in countries with cold winters. Antirrhinums, nasturtiums, pansies, primulas, violas and wallflowers are other examples of plants botanically perennial but treated as annuals in gardens in cooler climates.

Biennials such as foxgloves and hollyhocks can flower in their first season if sown in late winter indoors, but sown outdoors in early summer will flower the following year.

**Containers** may occupy key positions in the garden. So, to keep them looking good for a long period, tender summer annuals such as ageratum, nicotiana, petunia and salvia are highly recommended.

Children enjoy annuals, especially large and fast-growing nasturtiums and sunflowers. Be aware, though, that some seeds are potentially harmful, including corncockle and larkspur.

**Sowing** is the critical stage for hardy annuals, and the first step is to finely rake the soil surface. Although seeds can be broadcast and raked in, it is easier to spot weeds if several short parallel rows are used to make a patch of flowers. Straight veg garden-style rows work well. Sowing too early, when the soil is cold, is best avoided, and a late spring sowing into warm soil from which early-germinating weeds have been cleared is ideal. Fertilizer is unnecessary and makes hardy annuals leafy at the expense of flowers.

Autumn sowing is successful for many hardy annuals. Plants should be 'thinned' by discarding surplus plants so each remaining plant has enough space to develop.

# Bulbs

Used horticulturally, the term 'bulb' covers not only true bulbs such as narcissi and tulips, but also corms, rhizomes and tubers. Technically, the correct term for these underground plant organs is geophytes. They serve as an escape mechanism from adverse conditions such as very cold winters and very hot, dry summers.

Bulbs, like seeds, are compressed plants with everything they need to develop to full size. Being large compared to seeds, they mature very quickly and easily, making them highly suitable for temporary roles as houseplants, or for filling beds and containers, or gaps in summer borders.

Some bulbs are unreliable at persisting and have to be replaced each year. Others multiply and become valuable garden features.

Bulbs are underground stems with thickened fleshy leaves acting as storage organs. Supermarket onions are the most familiar bulbs, and ornamental onions (*Allium*) are also bulbs.

Rare and coveted bulbs can be expensive, but there are also plenty of low-cost bulbs usable for mass planting. This is possible because many bulbs can be field-grown mechanically, as with potatoes, and indeed with the same implements.

**Bulbs** that hide from winter include tulips and bulbous irises. These come from regions with very cold winters and hot, dry summers. They grow and flourish on water from winter snows or rains and then, having flowered, die back for the summer. In the garden they need fertile, moist spring soil and dry warm conditions after flowering.

**Tubers** are swollen rhizomes, for example potatoes, and while those are plants not generally thought of as ornamental people have grown the unusually floriferous '*Desire*' for its dainty blue flowers. Dahlias are another tuberous plant.

**Corms** are compressed underground stems. Crocus are the classic corm flower – whether the large, brightly coloured and unfortunately rather short-lived hybrids, or the persistent species such as *Crocus tommasinianus*. This has lilac or purple flowers in very early spring and commonly naturalizes. *Anemone blanda* and *A. nemorosa* also have corms and are fine bulbs for naturalizing.

**Rhizomes** are horizontal underground stems – many irises are rhizomatous. In cooler climates these are planted on or close to the surface, due to the nature of soil temperature, so they catch the sun's warmth.

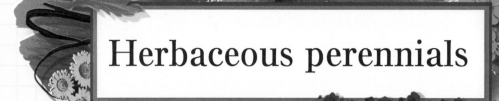

# Herbaceous perennials

Herbaceous perennials grow and flower in summer, then die down for the winter. Some very valuable perennials are almost shrubby; Russian sage (*Perovskia atriplicifolia*) is an example, with spires of blue flowers over fine, grey-green foliage, a most desirable plant for well-drained sunny gardens. These are sheared off at the end of winter and grow afresh.

Tall plants such as delphiniums are placed at the back of the border, although like all rules this one can be judiciously broken. Similarly early-flowering perennials such as *Anchusa azurea* 'Loddon Royalist', with its amazing blue flowers, and tall bearded irises are best at the back of the border. Moderately tall, later-emerging perennials such as phlox and *Veronicastrum virginicum* 'Fascination' can usefully obscure them when they have finished flowering.

Colour combinations can cause much anxiety, but most plants go well enough together. Where displeasing clashes occur, the spade and trowel will soon allow offending plants to be shifted to avoid recurrence the following year.

## Early perennials: *Geum*

'Totally Tangerine' produces masses of apricot-orange flowers, *Verbascum phoeniceum* 'Violetta' produces thin stems up to 75cm/30in tall of deep purple flowers from rosettes of dark green, heavily veined leaves.

## Midseason perennials: With

daylilies (*Hemerocallis*) each edible flower lasts just one day, but there are many bright trumpets over a long season in red, yellow and white, with strong strap-like foliage. *Anthemis tinctoria* 'E.C. Buxton' has ferny green foliage and masses of pale yellow daisy flowers.

## Late perennials: *Anemone × hybrida* 'Honorine

Jobert' grows to 1.5m/5ft and in early autumn carries abundant pure white flowers with yellow centres. *Phlox paniculata* 'Le Mahdi' has 1m/3¼ft stems bearing huge heads of fragrant violet flowers.

## Low perennials: *Euphorbia myrsinites*, with succulent blue-

green leaves and in spring acid green flowers, grows to 15cm/6in and is utterly drought-resistant. *Nepeta racemosa* 'Walker's Low' reaches 60cm/2ft and has deep mauve flowers and silvery-green scented leaves.

# Climbers

As mordern gardens become smaller the periphery, unless it is a hedge, is more and more often an opportunity for creativity and an important component of an enjoyable plant- and flower-rich space.

**House walls** do not always lend themselves to certain climbers. Precautions are often needed to keep the climber from damaging the house or to prevent the climber suffering when the house wall needs painting or pointing. Good fences are expensive and garden walls even more so. Building and designing boundaries and walls with planting in mind will make the most of costly structures.

In general terms, **sunny, south-facing** structures are easy to plant, west-, and, to a much lesser extent, east-facing ones offer good opportunities, but it must be said that north-facing can be a challenge.

**Trellis** in particular is a vital ingredient in small, modern gardens where a fence or wall is too harsh a division, and a hedge takes up too much space as well as maintenance. Trellis covered with plants is shallow and colourful in ways hedges seldom are, and makes charming divisions and screens. Also, by its porous nature, trellis filters breezes and avoids the turbulence associated with fences, walls and hedges.

Climbers for **south-facing:** With evergreen foliage and masses of starry white summer flowers, the Asiatic jasmines (*Trachelospermum asiaticum*) and confederate jasmines (*T. jasminoides*) are fine climbers for sunny, warm walls. *Campsis × tagliabuana* 'Madame Galen', a trumpet creeper, bears masses of spectacular orange-red 8cm/3in trumpets in late summer.

**Climbers for west-facing:**
*Jasminum officinale* 'Fiona Sunrise' is a vigorous yellow form of common jasmine producing small scented flowers in summer and gold autumn colour. *Solanum crispum* 'Glasnevin', or potato tree, is semi-evergreen and scrambles up trellis or wires, producing abundant scented violet-blue 2.5cm/1in flowers in summer.

**Climbers for east-facing structures:** *Akebia quinata* has handsome five-lobed leaves and scented purple spring flowers sometimes followed by edible purple sausage-shaped fruits. *Lonicera periclymenum* 'Graham Thomas' is a classic honeysuckle bearing dark green leaves with white undersides and scented white flowers that age to a charming brown-yellow, followed by red berries.

**Climbers for north-facing:**
The classic plant for sunless areas is climbing hydrangea (*Hydrangea anomala* subsp. *petiolaris*) which produces white lacecap hydrangea flowers and covers supports with basket-like stems. *Pileostegia viburnoides* climbs like a hydrangea but is evergreen and bears fluffy fingers of creamy flowers in summer.

# Ferns

Garden designers love ferns. They are often rich ingredients in flower-show gardens, and some of the most celebrated gardens feature whole beds of ferns. In garden centres, however, ferns are often relegated to a small, out-of-the-way area, and they rarely play a star role on websites or in catalogues. This could be because they are seen to lack the 'wow' factor. Another reason why ferns are undervalued is that most do not really do well in dry conditions, but this is only a problem in dry summers, and a bucket of water each week will see them through until the rains return. The water should be applied to the roots, not the foliage, to avoid causing the fronds to rot.

However, the unfurling of the **new foliage** in spring is as satisfying as flowers opening, and in damp summer weather, which is often only too common, ferns thrive and look gorgeously lush while the roses droop and shed petals.

Ferns are **undemanding** to **grow** if they can be provided with moist, shady, sheltered conditions and if the soil is improved by digging in a generous dressing of organic matter such as leaf mould.

Evergreen ferns include the creeping maidenhair fern (*Adiantum venustum*) from the Himalayas, which grows to 30cm/1ft and creeps to make a mat of ferny ground cover.

Robust ferns include the hart's tongue fern (*Asplenium scolopendrium*), which grows well in chalky soils that are sufficiently wet.

Those that will tolerate dry shade include *Dryopteris filix-mas* 'Linearis Polydactyla', 60cm/2ft, with thin wiry fronds.

Ferns for impact include the shuttlecock or ostrich fern (*Matteuccia struthiopteris*), 75cm/30in, with crozier-like unfurling spring shoots followed by typically shuttlecock-form fronds.

The bird's nest fern (*Asplenium nidus*) has long, brittle strap-shaped leaves in a circle like a nest, and is easy to grow in a shady humid area.

Tender ferns for indoors include the striking and surprisingly easy to grow staghorn fern (*Platycerium bifurcatum*), which loves a moist, cool shady room. Bathrooms can suit it well.

# Ground cover

Lawns are the traditional ground cover, but the work involved in keeping a lawn in good condition is daunting, especially when the lawn is in shade where good swards are hard to produce. Also banks and slopes are difficult and potentially unsafe to mow. Ground-cover plants that need tending perhaps just once or twice a year are a very tempting alternative. Most annual weeds will be suppressed by the ground cover itself and an associated mulch, although goose grass (*Galium aparine*) is an exception. Perennial weeds, however, will be an issue. Bindweed, with its vigorous climbing habit, is the bane of ground cover, though this form of planting is usually poor at dealing with perennial weeds generally. However, if they can be eradicated with a unplanted or fallow period, deep cultivation and use of weedkillers, and the newly planted ground cover mulched, then it can prove a very satisfying way of keeping a garden enjoyable. Coir matting is a good substitute for mulch on slopes where heavy rain will tend to strip off loose mulch.

**Ground cover for slopes:** spreading junipers are excellent for sunny slopes. *Juniperus squamata* 'Blue Carpet', with blue-grey needles, is particularly effective.

Pinning down **climbers** makes spectacular ground cover for slopes – clematis and climbing roses come to mind, but honeysuckles such as the evergreen *Lonicera japonica* 'Halliana' are also good.

**For sun:** Certain low-growing roses (about 60cm/2ft) lend themselves to this use, such as *Rosa* 'Kent' with lightly scented, double white flowers on disease-tolerant foliage and stems. *Persicaria affinis* 'Darjeeling Red' is one of the few effective herbaceous ground covers, as its stems and leaves dry to a most attractive red for autumn and winter colour.

**Under trees:** *Pachysandra terminalis*, a neat little evergreen related to box, makes a strong and robust ground cover, particularly for acid soils.

**Heather:** Where the soil is acid, in full sun and well-drained, try *Calluna vulgaris* 'Firefly', with red-brown foliage and purple-pink flowers.

**Herb lawns:** Creeping thymes are probably the best bet: *Thymus pulegioides* 'Aureus' with yellow leaves, white-flowered *T. serpyllum* 'Snowdrift' and *T. serpyllum* 'Pink Chintz' are good spreaders and have scented foliage.

Ground cover for **wild gardens** includes woodruff (*Galium odoratum*) and it is well named as it is a ruffian of a plant, colonizing ground even in unpromising dry shade. Common comfrey (*Symphytum officinale*) is also apt to spread, but in a wild ditch or hedge it is a bee-friendly plant and, if it gets out of hand, is readily cut and makes useful compost.

# Seasonal containers

Seasonal containers are all about growing. Growth is fast in summer and small plants make fine specimens by autumn, but since winter growth is very slight, good-sized plants must be used from the outset for winter pots. At the end of summer, tender plants must be discarded or kept in frost-free conditions until the following year. To save space, cuttings can be rooted in late summer and kept over winter.

In fact, the charm of seasonal containers is the opportunity to grow new, different and interesting things each year, particularly in summer when the choice is so very much greater than for winter displays.

Almost anything can be used, from clay pots to an old pair of wellington boots, but ideally the container will have excellent drainage and sufficient depth to hold plenty of moisture in summer.

Low-maintenance containers for summer include pelargoniums, which need minimal moisture and plenty of sun.

**Potting media** should not be coarse for summer containers, but in winter a fast-draining coarse potting medium is best. The water-retaining gel powders are of limited value and compost texture is the most important factor.

**Hanging baskets** have been revolutionized by trailing petunias and the closely related but smaller-flowered calibrachoa, both offering wide colour ranges from white through red to black.

Shade containers were traditionally planted with busy-lizzies, but disease problems have led these to be replaced with bedding fuchsias and fibrous-rooted begonias

**One-colour pots** always look good and neatly sidestep the problem of colour co-ordination. Try all-white tobacco flowers (*Nicotiana*), rich purple petunias or, for extroverts, double apricot begonias, which will certainly be hard to ignore. For spring, massed hyacinths and tulips are reliably delightful.

# Permanent containers

The natural home for containers is the patio. They are also great for framing doors and filling in alleys and other awkward spots. Permanent plants are naturally a little larger than seasonal plants, having considerable time to grow. Yet a container too large to move is well on the way to becoming a small border, so pots with a maximum diameter of 45–60cm/18–24in are advisable if movement is required. Repotting every other year and changing the top 5cm/2in of medium in years between repotting is wise to keep roots healthy.

**Soil-based** potting medium is heavy and therefore ideal for anchorage when taller plants such as trees are being grown in pots. Fortnightly feeding is usually required between mid-spring and early autumn.

**Trees** can be kept in containers as long as watering is well done – they will soon dry out even in a large pot. *Cercis siliquastrum* or Judas tree, with its pea-like flowers clustered unusually on older wood, birches (*Betula*) that cast light shade but have lovely bark and *Robinia × slavinii* 'Hillieri' with pink pea-flowers in early summer and casting light shade are good choices.

Permanent containers for sun can be based on warmth-loving **evergreen shrubs**. Olives and pittosporum are good choices.

*Pittosporum tenuifolium* 'Silver Queen', *P. tenuifolium* 'Warnham Gold' (yellow) and also black *P. tenuifolium* 'Tom Thumb' can be **clipped with ease** and lend themselves to containers. But, like olives, moving them to shelter in winter is wise in cold regions.

Using pot feet to ensure an air gap to prevent roots reaching the soil is wise. Otherwise, pots can be shifted at least once a year to break any newly formed roots.

### Aquatic containers

can hold a small water lily such as *Nymphaea tetragona* with its white, mildly scented cup-shaped 5cm/2in flowers in summer. Just 15–30cm/6–12in of water will suffice.

For **permanent containers** in shade, evergreens such as *Garrya elliptica* with its long catkins (in male cultivars such as 'James Roof'), glossy camellias with the bonus of spring flowers, and the rather less usual mountain laurel (*Kalmia latifolia*) with waxy, cup-shaped flowers give good results.

# Japanese maples

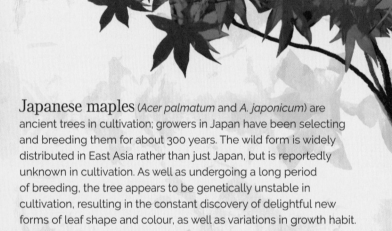

Japanese maples (*Acer palmatum* and *A. japonicum*) are ancient trees in cultivation; growers in Japan have been selecting and breeding them for about 300 years. The wild form is widely distributed in East Asia rather than just Japan, but is reportedly unknown in cultivation. As well as undergoing a long period of breeding, the tree appears to be genetically unstable in cultivation, resulting in the constant discovery of delightful new forms of leaf shape and colour, as well as variations in growth habit.

For some reason, Japanese maples are considered hard to grow yet this cannot be the case given their widespread cultivation and the many hundreds of cultivars recorded. Acid soil is not needed but they do require a soil that drains well in winter and does not dry out too much in summer – although on a garden scale a soak every two weeks should see those that are well established in the soil through dry periods. Wet, compacted clay or gravelly sands will need improving with careful cultivation and generous organic matter before planting. Leaves can scorch and fall in hot, dry weather if the tree is in full sun, but a new set is generally grown by autumn. Frosted leaves are also a risk, so cover young spring foliage with fleece or old net curtains. Needless to say, shelter from autumn gales is sensible if the colourful autumn leaves are not to go flying.

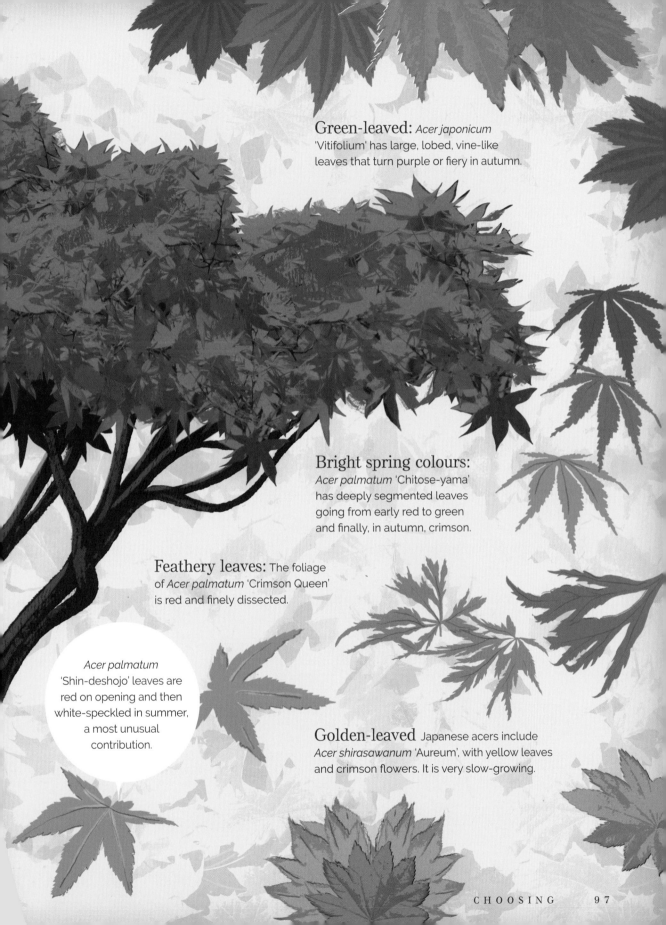

**Green-leaved:** *Acer japonicum* 'Vitifolium' has large, lobed, vine-like leaves that turn purple or fiery in autumn.

**Bright spring colours:** *Acer palmatum* 'Chitose-yama' has deeply segmented leaves going from early red to green and finally, in autumn, crimson.

**Feathery leaves:** The foliage of *Acer palmatum* 'Crimson Queen' is red and finely dissected.

*Acer palmatum* 'Shin-deshojo' leaves are red on opening and then white-speckled in summer, a most unusual contribution.

**Golden-leaved** Japanese acers include *Acer shirasawanum* 'Aureum', with yellow leaves and crimson flowers. It is very slow-growing.

# Crab apples

Cherries have perhaps the most spectacular spring blossom, but ornamental or crab apples come close behind. They are also scented, notably *Malus coronaria* var. *dasycalyx* 'Charlottae', said to be reminiscent of violets. Crab apples are also more versatile with, in many cases, fine autumn foliage and highly decorative autumn and early winter fruits.

Versatility is one reason for their value in the garden, but so is size. They tend to be modest (for a tree), at about 5–7m/16–23ft in height. With several species and many cultivars available, crab apples are highly varied and gardeners have a broad choice that can fill many gardening situations.

These trees thrive in any good, well-drained soil and give an orchard-type, country feel to less formal gardens but also look effective as centrepieces in beds and borders. They need plenty of sun and will not thrive in shade. While root disease can be very damaging in wet soils, planting on a slight mound can often reduce the risk in gardens where the soil lies wet in winter or for a long time after rain at other seasons. Although they suffer from the same pests and diseases as edible apples, crab apples can often pollinate dessert and cooking apples. Indeed 'Golden Hornet' is used in commercial orchards for this purpose.

**Shrubby** and small in size: *Malus baccata* 'Street Parade' is a form of Siberian crab apple with bright red fruits on a compact plant.

**Good** for **fruits:** *Malus × robusta* 'Red Sentinel' produces glossy bright red crab apples.

Resistant to **scab disease:** *Malus* 'Rudolph' has an upright, narrow habit with rose flowers and elongated, pendent orange-yellow fruits.

**Purple leaves:** *Malus* 'Royalty' turns red in autumn and carries dark red fruits.

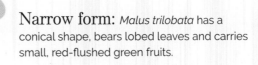

**Narrow form:** *Malus trilobata* has a conical shape, bears lobed leaves and carries small, red-flushed green fruits.

# Ornamental grasses

For some people, only colourful blooms will do, but ornamental grasses have a beauty of their own, one that often sets off their more showy flowers and, of course, they have a very long season of interest. Some are evergreen and last over winter, while others are deciduous and take on autumn shades. In both cases, young spring foliage followed by flowers and then seed heads provide interest almost all year round. Deciduous grasses are cut back each spring before new shoots grow enough to be harmed by trimming. Evergreen leaves can be left, and any dead material simply pulled out with a gloved hand.

Some grasses grow from late winter and are best planted in autumn: *Deschampsia*, *Festuca*, *Helictotrichon* and *Stipa*. Others grow in late spring when the soil and air warms, and are much better planted in late spring than other seasons: *Miscanthus*, *Panicum* and *Pennisetum*.

For convenience, sedges and rushes, *Carex* and *Luzula* for example, are also combined horticulturally speaking into grasses although they are very different botanically.

Most grasses need good sunlight and a reasonably fertile, well-drained soil. Fertility can produce excess growth and poor form, so feeding needs to be done with discretion and a light hand.

**For containers:** New Zealand wind grass (*Anemanthele lessoniana*) with colourful, arching autumn foliage.

**For shade:** *Hakonechloa macra* 'Aureola' has pale yellow foliage, ideal for brightening up dark spots.

**For flowers:** *Pennisetum alopecuroides* 'Herbstzauber' carries fluffy green-white flowers in tall plumes.

**Variegated:** *Miscanthus sinensis* 'Morning Light' – tall, with white-edged leaves and pink autumn flowers.

**Colourful:** Japanese blood grass (*Imperata cylindrica* 'Rubra') is, as might be expected, deep red in foliage colour.

**From seed:** foxtail barley (*Hordeum jubatum*) carries silvery, feathery plumes that are highly mobile in a breeze.

**Giant grasses** for impact: *Arundo donax* or giant reed is 3m/10ft, with bamboo-like stems.

**Ground-cover grasses:** *Festuca glauca* 'Elijah Blue' has cushions of spiky blue leaves and taller, blue, late-summer flowers.

# Roses

More than 15,000 named roses
have been recorded, but of course most have lapsed
into obscurity. leaving a core of well-established cultivars that
constitute the mainstay of rose production and planting. From the considerable
number of new cultivars introduced each year, only a few join the standard
repertoire of garden roses – a repertoire that contains arguably the best-loved
of all garden plants.

**Rose-growing** is unfortunately dominated by fungal blackspot disease,
and the rose's tolerance (complete long-term resistance is unknown) can
clinch its success as a garden variety. As fungicides have been withdrawn, the
natural resistance of roses has become more important and now breeders
place this very high on their list of priorities.

The **rose border** was in its time a very popular thing of beauty but
required much pruning, deadheading and spraying to keep off pests. The
sulphur dioxide pollution of the last century, due to use of coal as fuel,
was reportedly effective against disease. With cleaner air, disease has
become more severe.

An important point is that
roses will seldom thrive if planted
immediately after a previous rose
on the same site. This is called
replant disease, and can be avoided
by changing the soil or planting
elsewhere.

For cutting:
*Rosa* 'Ispahan' is a
vigorous shrub rose with
old-fashioned, highly
scented double
pink flowers.

Thornless or nearly so:
*Rosa* 'Zéphirine Drouhin',
an old climbing rose, bears
double, deep pink flowers all
summer, and it even puts up
with north-facing walls.

For hedges:
*Rosa* 'Charles de Mills'
produces double, crimson,
lightly scented flowers in
midsummer, while *R.* 'Roseraie
de l'Haÿ' offers crimson-purple
flowers all through summer.

For ground-cover:
*Rosa* 'Grouse', a vigorous,
prostrate variety, is covered in
delicate white flowers like wild
roses, followed by red hips. It is
great for banks and to grow into
unfavourable places.

# Indoor plants

Indoor environments can be challenging to many plants, being rather dark and with a dry atmosphere. Central heating in particular dries out the atmosphere, stressing plants as moisture is pulled out of them into the dry air faster than it can be replenished by the roots. Unfortunately, the usual reaction to stressed plants is to water them, which tends to be fatal. Warm rooms are much more stressful to plants than cool ones. Freezing rooms and fluctuating temperatures, near radiators for example, are even worse.

Flowering **houseplants:** Moth orchids (*Phalaenopsis*) grow well in bright, sunny, heated rooms and often produce flower spikes in succession.

A **porch** or sunroom with heat in summer and high light levels will suit succulents such as *Agave parryi*. With rosettes of blue-tinged grey leaves and black spines along the leaf edge, this is a striking choice.

Plants for **sunny conservatories:** As long as the worst frost is excluded, succulents such as *Agave americana*, with sculptural, spiny-edged grey-green leaves, will thrive.

Luckily there are plants that can take tolerate indoor conditions and render homes, hospitals, offices and schools much more pleasant. There is even evidence that the presence of greenery and flowers induces good health, happiness and also productivity. Even more interestingly, indoor plants – or perhaps the microbes in the growing media – absorb the pollutants inevitable with modern furnishing and building methods, rendering them harmless.

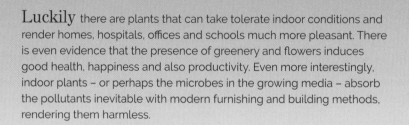

Plants for humid bathrooms and steamy kitchens: *Tillandsia cyanea* is a bromeliad or pineapple family plant, with rosettes of narrow, dark green leaves and hand-like bunches of pink and green flowers.

Plants for sunny windowsills: Gardenia (*Gardenia jasminoides*) has glossy evergreen leaves and highly fragrant, trumpet-shaped white flowers 8cm/3in across.

Plants for darker rooms: *Zamioculcas zamiifolia* has clumps of strangely succulent, almost bamboo-like green stems with leaflets arranged each side.

Plants for shade: *Schefflera actinophylla*, with upright habit, has shoots that terminate in hand-like clusters.

# Wisteria

Wisteria is a hugely popular climber, with twining stems and, all being well, abundant drooping heads of fragrant flowers in spring. Native to North America and East Asia, wisteria belongs to the legume or pea family, and in gardens tends to be unruly. Dwarf wisteria is unknown, and these climbers need ample space to spread. They will even ascend tall trees, flowering very freely in the canopies, with no apparent harm to either tree or climber. Some species climb clockwise, typically *Wisteria floribunda*, others, like *W. sinensis*, anticlockwise. It is unclear why they do this.

**Leaves** and **flowers** come out simultaneously on *Wisteria floribunda*, it is best displayed in trees or on pergolas, where the very long flower trusses can hang clear of the leaves and be enjoyed for their spectacular beauty.

*Wisteria sinensis* and its cultivars **produce flowers** before the leaves emerge and are especially eye-catching when grown on walls and structures.

When **grown from seed**, wisterias do not come true to type and neither do they flower quickly, although most will begin to bloom after 7–12 years.

Although those grown into **tall trees** neither get nor need pruning, other wisterias are best pruned twice a year: once in late summer to shorten all the new shoots (which means more flower buds on the remaining spur), and again in late winter to remove all the surplus new shoots that might obscure the flowers.

In **smaller gardens** the house wall is the commonest destination for wisteria, but they will need to be prevented from invading and damaging gutters and tiles.

Wisteria to **stand alone:** *Wisteria floribunda* 'Yae-kokuryu' (black dragon) has fragrant violet-blue flowers.

Wisteria **for scent:** *Wisteria sinensis* 'Amethyst', deep violet with a yellow centre.

Wisteria **for trees:** *Wisteria floribunda* 'Multijuga' is vigorous and carries very long fragrant lilac flower racemes.

# Clematis

Like roses, clematis are richly coloured and potentially spectacular. While there are very worthwhile herbaceous clematis it is the climbers that are especially relished; to adorn trellis, fences, walls and wigwams they arguably have no equal.

They are **inexpensive** to buy, due to the ease of growth and readiness to root from cuttings. A strong new plant can form in as little as 18 months. While they are sometimes short-lived it is easy to raise more from cuttings, or from seed for species.

Probably the **easiest clematis** are *Clematis montana* and its cultivars, which grow strongly.

*Clematis tangutica*, especially 'Bill MacKenzie', is another **strong grower** able to colonize tall structures and engulf eyesores and small trees. It has silky seed heads that sparkle in frosts until spring.

At the **other end** of the scale, *Clematis alpina*, including its violet-flowered cultivar 'Frances Rivis', and *Clematis texensis*, with tulip-shaped flowers, are dainty little climbers for smaller gardens, although they are not long-flowering.

Such is the demand for **compact clematis** that new 'patio clematis' have been bred. These are compact yet long-flowering and floriferous like the larger garden hybrids and robust, growing well even in pots.

Garden hybrids have larger flowers and include some well-known favourites such as 'Nelly Moser' with lilac flowers that can be 20cm/8in wide and 'The President' with violet-purple flowers up to 18cm/7in across.

Evergreen clematis include *Clematis cirrhosa*. The variety of 'Wisley Cream', has small creamy bell-like flowers in winter and ferny foliage. It climbs to 3m/10ft or more and is ideal for sheltered walls.

# Ericaceous plants

In acid soils iron is much more available to plants. Camellias, heathers and rhododendrons are common examples of plants that are 'acid-loving' or ericaceous. Although these plants cannot be readily grown in alkaline soils they thrive in acidic potting media.

Many **originated in forests** and grew in the moist acidic leafmould soils in low light conditions. By happy chance these conditions are common in gardens, especially small ones, and ericaceous shrubs such as camellia, pieris and rhododendrons are excellent choices for container cultivation. Being mostly evergreen, they provide year-round greenery in even the smallest, shadiest garden.

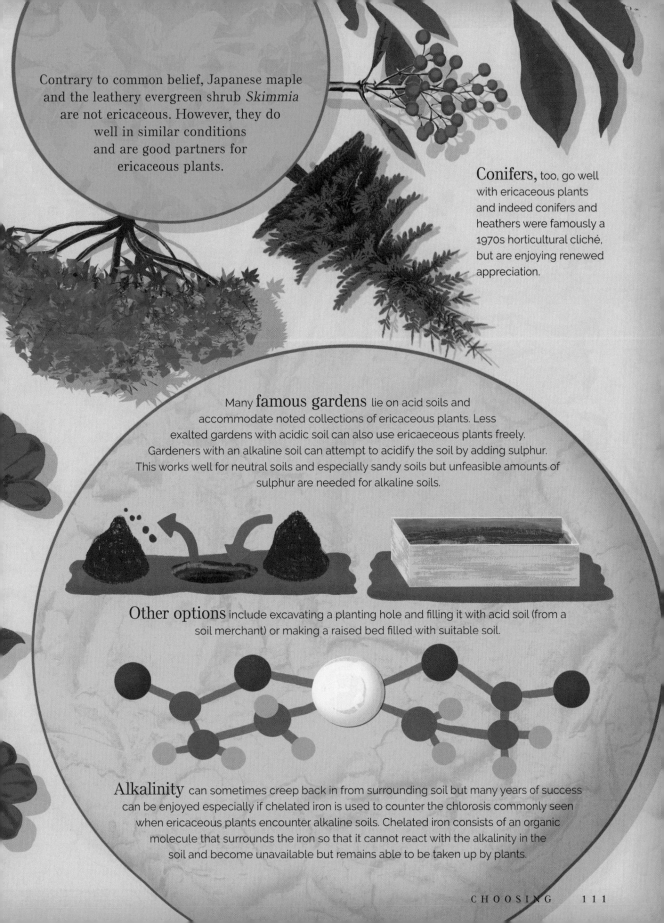

Contrary to common belief, Japanese maple and the leathery evergreen shrub *Skimmia* are not ericaceous. However, they do well in similar conditions and are good partners for ericaceous plants.

**Conifers,** too, go well with ericaceous plants and indeed conifers and heathers were famously a 1970s horticultural cliché, but are enjoying renewed appreciation.

Many **famous gardens** lie on acid soils and accommodate noted collections of ericaceous plants. Less exalted gardens with acidic soil can also use ericaeceous plants freely. Gardeners with an alkaline soil can attempt to acidify the soil by adding sulphur. This works well for neutral soils and especially sandy soils but unfeasible amounts of sulphur are needed for alkaline soils.

**Other options** include excavating a planting hole and filling it with acid soil (from a soil merchant) or making a raised bed filled with suitable soil.

**Alkalinity** can sometimes creep back in from surrounding soil but many years of success can be enjoyed especially if chelated iron is used to counter the chlorosis commonly seen when ericaceous plants encounter alkaline soils. Chelated iron consists of an organic molecule that surrounds the iron so that it cannot react with the alkalinity in the soil and become unavailable but remains able to be taken up by plants.

# Vegetables
# & Herbs

# Site and planning

Any reasonably fertile, well-drained soil in full sun is suitable for herbs and vegetables. Poorly drained areas can be greatly improved by building raised beds.

Herbs generally need low levels of fertility, though there are exceptions, for best flavour. Vegetables however, perform best at high levels of fertility. Improving fertility by adding manure, garden compost and any other well-rotted organic matter is very effective both before setting up a herb and vegetable plot and at intervals, ideally at least every three years.

Checking the pH and adding lime to bring the pH to about 7.5 (slightly alkaline) helps suppress soil diseases such as club root of cabbages and parsnip canker.

Good light is particularly important for herbs as far as flavour goes and they should have the sunniest position even if this means pots around the back door. Fresh herbs are expensive to buy and homegrown ones are markedly superior as they are of course very much fresher. It is worth giving them the best treatment.

Unfortunately vegetables won't grow well in significant shade, but where the shade is partial or light, vegetables, particular beetroot, peas, salads and runner beans are feasible.

**The rotation of crops** by growing a particular type of crop on a different piece of ground each year helps to avoid the build-up of crop-specific diseases in the soil. A typical rotation is Year 1 Potatoes and tomatoes, Year 2 Legumes, roots and onion tribe, Year 3 Cabbage tribe or brassicas. Everything else can go where convenient.

**Weed clearance** is essential and can be done with herbicides, covering the ground with black plastic for a summer or primary cultivation or digging.

Primary tillage is the breaking up of soil to at least 15cm (6in) and generally involves digging or rotovating.

Secondary cultivation is the raking and treading used to get a firm, level seedbed.

Vegetables can easily be raised in containers filled with a peat-free growing medium on a sunny patio.

Raised beds should be no more than about 1–1.2m/3¼ –4 ft across so the whole surface can be reached from the sides.

Water supplies nearby are almost essential when growing vegetables.

Shelter in windy spots by a fence or a hedge intercepting prevailing winds is usually very beneficial as long as it does not cast excess shade.

Service areas such as compost bins, sheds, places to store canes, stakes and netting are all good investments.

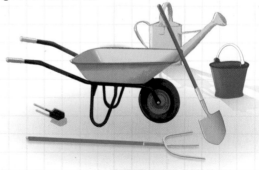

Tools can be quite limited, with a fork, hoe, rake, trowel and spade being sufficient. You will also need a bucket, watering can and wheelbarrow.

# Seeds and sowing

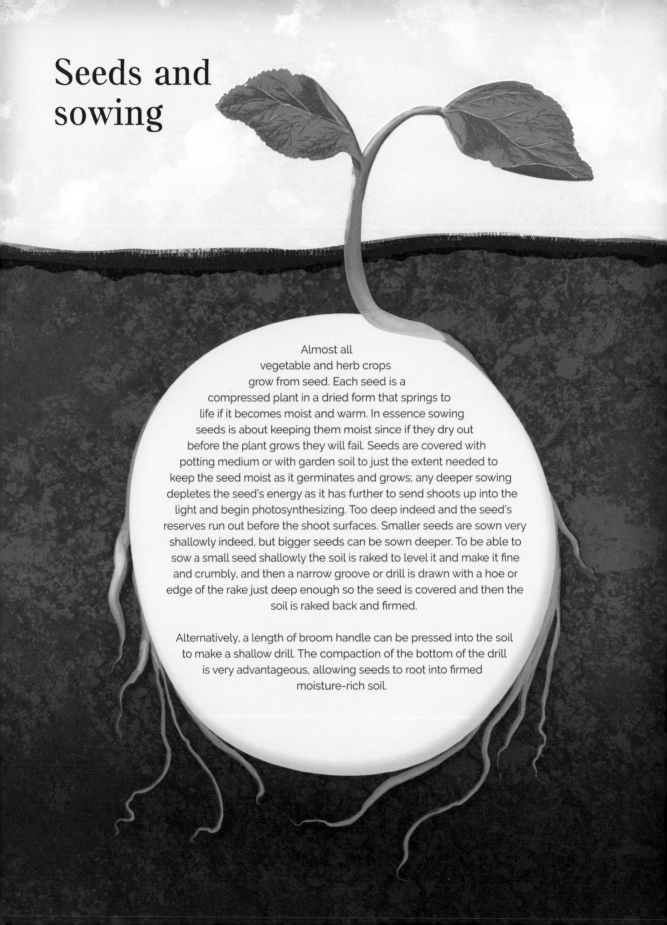

Almost all
vegetable and herb crops
grow from seed. Each seed is a
compressed plant in a dried form that springs to
life if it becomes moist and warm. In essence sowing
seeds is about keeping them moist since if they dry out
before the plant grows they will fail. Seeds are covered with
potting medium or with garden soil to just the extent needed to
keep the seed moist as it germinates and grows; any deeper sowing
depletes the seed's energy as it has further to send shoots up into the
light and begin photosynthesizing. Too deep indeed and the seed's
reserves run out before the shoot surfaces. Smaller seeds are sown very
shallowly indeed, but bigger seeds can be sown deeper. To be able to
sow a small seed shallowly the soil is raked to level it and make it fine
and crumbly, and then a narrow groove or drill is drawn with a hoe or
edge of the rake just deep enough so the seed is covered and then the
soil is raked back and firmed.

Alternatively, a length of broom handle can be pressed into the soil
to make a shallow drill. The compaction of the bottom of the drill
is very advantageous, allowing seeds to root into firmed
moisture-rich soil.

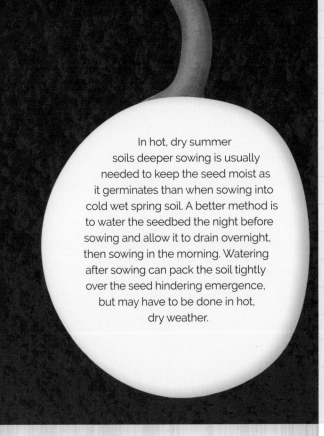

In hot, dry summer soils deeper sowing is usually needed to keep the seed moist as it germinates than when sowing into cold wet spring soil. A better method is to water the seedbed the night before sowing and allow it to drain overnight, then sowing in the morning. Watering after sowing can pack the soil tightly over the seed hindering emergence, but may have to be done in hot, dry weather.

**Warmth** can be provided when sowing indoors, ideally by a heated propagator. Outdoors a sudden cold, and/or wet period after sowing can be fatal to the seeds, and re-sowing may be required.

**Seeds deteriorate quickly** if stored in a warm or humid place. However, stored cool and dry they may remain viable for years. An airtight container with some silica gel drying agent placed in a cool spot, ideally in a refrigerator, is good practice.

celeriac

leek

apple

brassica

**F1 hybrid seeds** are more expensive but often their great vigour, uniformity and yield is generally worthwhile, especially with celery, celeriac, brassicas, parsnips, tomatoes and sweetcorn. Their merits are arguably less clear for carrots and leeks and cheaper open-pollinated seed is worth considering.

carrot

brassica

celery

parsnip

sweetcorn

# Plant raising

Vegetables and herbs are very easy to grow, as long as they become established well from seed or transplants. If this crucial stage is successful subsequent growing is straightforward.

A wide range of herb and vegetable plants is offered in catalogues and garden centres to transplant into the garden in spring. They are an excellent way of establishing the garden each year, but it is cheaper and very enjoyable to raise plants from seed at home.

Usually seed is sown indoors either in shallow pots (pans) or in seedtrays and the seedlings are set out into individual containers as is commonly done for tomatoes. Alternatively cell or module trays are used with one or several seeds per cell. The plants grow in the cell until they are ready to be planted out.

Good-quality seed and potting media are crucial for success. Cheap unknown brands might not give the best results. However, growing, bag medium, tipped out of the bags and used for potting up, is good for potting vegetables and relatively inexpensive.

**Watering little** and **often** is ideal for transplants. Drought stress will greatly slow growth and compromise root health. However, tomatoes can be slightly stressed to advantage as this promotes flowers and an early crop.

**Pest and disease control is** very necessary, particularly of greenfly or aphids as these spread viruses that are very damaging to young plants.

**Cell-tray raised plants** are set out as soon as the roots bind the compost and should be well watered before and after planting.

It is vital that seedlings are not overcrowded or they get excessively tall and thin (drawn).

Roots should be confined to the pots and cells, by means of an air gap between the containers and their supports or the ground. Alternatively, slightly moving them each week will prevent significant rooting.

**Tender transplants,** such as tomatoes and peppers, require a prolonged growing period in heated conditions.

It is **worth considering** if buying these plants from a nursery might be more convenient and indeed cheaper if much heating has to be used.

# Buying plants

Nurseries and garden suppliers provide a wide range of vegetable and herb transplants for gardeners. For uncertain gardeners and ones short of space to raise plants these are very helpful. Even though seed is usually cheaper, where only a few plants are wanted it is not much more expensive to buy plants than seeds. Typically gardeners only need one or two examples of many herbs. However, basil and parsley are often wanted in larger quantities and cell trays are good value compared to individual pots.

Small 9-10cm/3½-4in diameter pots provide a strong plant ideal for herbs, which the gardener can gather lightly from soon after planting. Also plants that need to do a lot of growing in short frost-free summer season are very advantageously bought in pots. Aubergine, chilli, sweet peppers and tomatoes are examples of these.

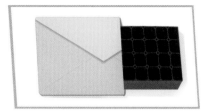

**Smaller plants** are supplied in cell trays and these are available either by mail-order or from retail outlets.

Order **catalogue plants** well in advance as there is a temptation among suppliers to sow more rather too late to supply tardy orders.

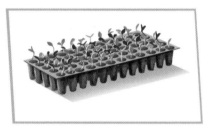

**Plug trays** of very tiny plants can be bought and these are planted into small pots on receipt.

In fact all **bought plants** are best placed in good growing conditions or potted up as soon as possible after delivery.

**Grafted plants,** where a productive high-quality scion (upper part) is cut and placed in extremely careful proximity to similarly cut rootstock of a highly vigorous and disease-resistant cultivar, grow into a plant with all the advantages of both segments.

**Importing trouble** to your garden is not impossible and all bought-in plants should be inspected for pests and disease. Replacements should be sought for any suspect plants. Typically, whitefly, red spider mites and thrips can be encountered.

# Plant care

Happily, herb and vegetable plants are not very demanding to care for. They should not get too dry, nor should feeding be neglected and they should be planted in plenty of light.

It is usually wise **when sowing outdoors** to sow rather more seeds than you need for the desired final number of plants.

It is **good practice** to thoroughly water dry soil before sowing or planting, allowing a few hours for it to drain.

If **emergence is good**, remove the surplus, a process called thinning. Sometimes the thinnings can be used in salads and sometimes they can be carefully lifted with a trowel and replanted to fill in any gaps, which is often referred to as 'gapping-up'.

Even where **seeds and plants** go into moist soil they will need initial watering to keep the soil around their roots moist.

After a **week or two** they will take root into the moist soil and find moisture by using their roots to explore the soil.

30cm
1 ft

**In dry spells** maturing plants can deplete soil moisture in 10–14 days. Plants are robust and will survive until harvest in almost all cases without watering but a soak of the top 30cm/1ft every two weeks will greatly improve yield and quality.

**Hoeing** is the main weed control method. Push-pull hoes are quick and accurate and bring up few weed seeds from deeper in the soil.

**Draw hoes** use a chopping action and work better in wet soils or where large weeds are encountered.

**Mulching** with bark, compost or black plastic, ideally biodegradable, sheets is highly effective at controlling weeds and conserving water.

**Either liquid** and **solid** fertilizers can be used; the latter are cheaper and less work. Ideally a base dressing is applied before planting and sowing, with top-dressing as needed through the life of the crop.

# Harvesting

Timely harvesting is important in getting the best out of the investment in growing a crop of vegetables. All too often there is a glut when crops mature in a rush, perhaps due to sudden heatwave. Logically, growing slightly less than you expect to need and topping up from the supermarket would make sense. This however sits uneasily with many growers who must therefore resign themselves to waste, or develop culinary skills to utilize surplus produce – lettuce and courgette soups spring to mind.

As harvest approaches a close eye has to be kept on the maturing produce as it is not only the grower who finds it attractive. Jays, mice and pigeons will strip broad beans and peas, squirrels are partial to sweetcorn and slugs and snails mistake lettuce hearts for places to seek sanctuary from their many enemies and a safe place to graze.

Crops do not mature evenly and picking over the maturing crop taking each edible part as it falls ready will reduce spoilage and often induce the plant to ripen or fill out the remaining pods, or fruits in the case of fruiting vegetables. Any damaged or substandard ones can be discarded at this stage or quickly processed – bolting or flowering onions, for example, can be used 'green' in the kitchen.

**Root vegetables**, cabbages, pumpkin, winter squash and vegetable marrow can be kept indoors in frost-free conditions

**Clamps or pies** are low-cost outdoor stores where produce such as potatoes and root vegetables are stacked on a well-drained area of soil, covered with straw and then at least 15cm/6in of soil with sloping sides patted smooth with the back of the spade to shed the rain.

**Root cellars** are used for the same purpose as clamps in very cold regions with severe winters such as Canada and Germany.

Preserving **surplus vegetables** by pickling, chutneys or other preserves is well worth planning for.

**Continuity of supply** is assured by sowing at suitable intervals, known as 'successional sowing', so crops mature in sequence without gaps in supply. Unfortunately the weather can sometimes upset even the best plans.

**Residues of crops** can carry over pests and diseases to the next crop and are best removed smartly after harvest and composted unless infested, when they are best burnt, buried or consigned to the municipal green waste service. There industrial composting will render all pests, diseases and indeed weed seeds harmless.

# Salads

Although lettuces are deservedly the most popular salad, other crops are very worthwhile too: chard, chicory, herbs, land cress, leaf beet, endive, kale, Oriental greens, radicchio, rocket, sorrel and spinach. Ready-prepared supermarket salads can offer inspiration, as the components of these mixtures are easy to grow.

Salads are easily grown. Sowing direct in the ground from early spring until late summer is usually possible, although sowing in containers is also an option. Most respond well to raising in cell trays and planting out later.

Sowing a short, perhaps 1.5m/5ft row, of salads is sufficient for a week's supply. As salads don't remain long in good condition frequent sowing, usually every three weeks is advisable to minimize periods of over and under supply.

Thinnings can be used for mini-leaves. Alternatively, denser sowings may be made purposely for mini-leaf salads: allow 15cm/6in between rows and 1cm/½in between plants.

These small plants are ideal for intercropping or growing between a widely spaced slower-growing crop such as brussels sprouts – see p133.

Leaves are gathered when the plant is about 8cm/3in tall, leaving a stump for a second or more cuttings. These are especially useful when space is limited and also during winter when hearted lettuce, for example, can be difficult to induce to form hearts.

In hot, dry weather, watering every 10 days, applying about two watering cans' worth every 1sq m/1.2 sq yd, prevents bolting.

Radishes (brassicas) and salad onions are also important salads.

Butterhead lettuces, soft round hearts, very easy to grow, medium flavour.

Little Gem: sweet crunchy mini-hearts ideal for small gardens.

Crispheads including icebergs or 'Webbs': crisp leaves and tolerant of dry, hot weather.

Stem lettuce (celtuce) – grown for its cooked stems, cultivation is as for other lettuce.

# Onion tribe

The onion tribe includes garlic, leeks, onions and shallots, all of which are easy to grow, if you choose the right methods. While onions are cheap to buy, garlic, leeks, and shallots are often disproportionately expensive.

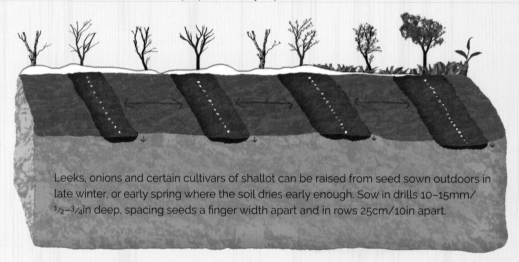

Leeks, onions and certain cultivars of shallot can be raised from seed sown outdoors in late winter, or early spring where the soil dries early enough. Sow in drills 10–15mm/ ½–¾in deep, spacing seeds a finger width apart and in rows 25cm/10in apart.

## Sowing indoors in cell trays
is more reliable, sowing either two seeds per small cell and singling plants later if necessary or sowing six or seven seeds per larger cell to get a clump of four to five plants.

## Garlic and shallots are usually
raised from sets. Onion sets too are very widely used, being especially easy to grow. Sets are small bulbs that are planted where they are to crop.

**The onion tribe** need full sun and fertile, well-drained soil, that is not acid. Ideally add organic matter and general fertilizer before sowing. Top-dressing with nitrogen-rich fertilizer is usually helpful, especially for leeks and onions.

Onion types: round, elongated, brown, red, yellow, white skins.

Shallot types: round, elongated, brown, red,

Garlic types: softneck , hardneck , elephant garlic.

Leek types: Autumn and winter, thick pot leeks usually grown for competitions.

Herb alliums such as chives and Welsh onions are very useful back-garden crops for flavour and garnish.

# Carrot tribe and
# other root vegetables

Carrots, celeriac, parsnips and indeed parsley, both herb types and the Hamburg types grown for edible roots, are biennials, forming a fleshy root in the first year and flowering in the second. Celery is also a biennial which forms a sturdy plant but has little root. Florence fennel is technically a perennial although grown as an annual.

Any friable well-drained, moderately fertile garden soil in sun will support carrots, as long as it is not acid. Removing as many stones as possible helps to reduce forked roots. Although there is little evidence that adding organic matter causes forked roots it is best avoided, except for beetroot.

Beetroot, celeriac and celery require very fertile soils and respond well to fertilizers. Florence fennel, parsnips, salsify and scorzonera need moderate fertility. Carrots and other roots seldom require fertilizer.

Sow these crops in 10–15mm/½–¾in deep drills, spacing seeds about a finger width apart. Celeriac and celery are best raised from early spring sowings made indoors to plant out in early summer. Florence fennel is sometimes tricky and an early Summer sowing is usually best, yielding autumn crops.

Sow, or for celeriac, celery and fennel, plant out, in rows 20cm/10in apart for early carrots and 30cm/12in apart for most other crops but for the best celeriac and parsnips allow 45cm/18in.

**Early carrots**, bolt-resistant beetroot and parsnips are sown from early spring. For carrots, beetroot, Hamburg parsley, salsify and scorzonera, a mid-spring sowing is made for later lifting. Later sowing can be made for carrots and beetroot for lifting from late summer.

Seedlings should be **thinned as soon as possible**, to about 10cm/4in apart, 15cm/6in for beetroot, winter carrots and parsnips.

**Watering** is usually unnecessary, but in really dry spells a thorough soak every ten days will help swell the crop. Celeriac, celery and Florence fennel are injured by dry spells and are best watered every week.

**Carrots, celeriac, celery** and **Florence fennel** can be used as soon as bulbs, heads or roots are a worthwhile size. Beetroot, carrots and celeriac can be lifted and stored in boxes of soil or sand for winter use. Better-flavoured carrots usually result from covering the crop with a frost-excluding layer of cardboard topped with polythene sheeting to shed rain. This is satisfactory for other root crops too: parsnips, salsify and scorzonera.

**Carrot fly**
will damage carrot, celeriac, celery, Hamburg parsley and parsnip roots. Covering with insect-proof mesh will exclude this pest.

Carrot, fennel and parsley foliage is too light to suppress weeds, so careful hand-weeding and hoeing is required.

# Cabbage tribe

Mild, wet climates very much suit the cabbage tribe or brassicas, and they mostly crop abundantly. Typical crops include cabbage, cauliflowers, calabrese, Chinese broccoli, Chinese cabbage, Brussels sprouts, kale, kale sprouts, kohl rabi, Oriental greens, savoy cabbage, turnips, sprouting broccoli and swedes.

A skilled gardener in a mild region with sufficient space can have cabbages and calabrese every month of the year, a feat of which only lettuce is capable and then only if greenhouse grown in winter.

**Raising plants** from pots or cell trays is trouble-free if they are covered with fleece or insect-proof mesh before and after planting out to exclude pests. When the seedling roots bind the potting medium firmly together it is time to plant out. Water the transplants before and after planting up to the depth of the lowest leaves. Press the soil around the plant roots to make sure it is very firm.

**Cabbage patches** usually have to be netted against pigeons.

Any fertile **garden soil** in a sunny spot is suitable. Add rotted manure or other organic matter and a base dressing of fertilizer about two weeks before planting.

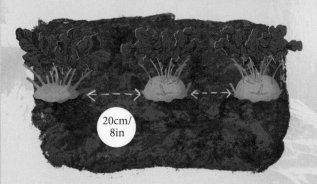

Many **brassica plants** grow very large, Brussels sprouts, kale, kale sprouts and sprouting broccoli for example, and are widely spaced at least 75cm/30in each way.

Others are **quite small:** kohl rabi, Chinese cabbage and other Oriental brassicas, winter radish and turnips can be grown in rows 30cm/12in apart allowing 20cm/10in between rows and plants respectively.

Swedes, turnips and winter radish can be lifted and stored indoors in boxes of soil or sand to avoid frost. Certain cabbages, both red and white, are available for storage indoors which can be useful in prolonged freezes.

**Chinese cabbage** can be stored for many weeks in the salad compartment of the refrigerator.

**Pests include** cabbage root fly, caterpillars and mealy cabbage aphid, which can be excluded with insect-proof mesh. Card collars at the base of plants can reduce cabbage root fly losses.

# Peas and beans

Beans and peas, grouped as legumes, are much less productive in terms of yield than, say, root crops or brassicas, but are especially protein-rich.

Runner beans are the exception, in terms of yield, being very productive indeed due to their long cropping season, typical of tender perennials which is what they are. This goes far to explain why they are so very widely grown.

Broad and French beans and also peas are annuals. The beans and peas, and indeed any edible pods, are well, if subtly, flavoured. Chickpeas and soya beans are sometimes grown, the latter particularly for their immature edible pods served as edamame. Asparagus pea and lablab beans are curiosities which while edible are perhaps more valued for their ornamental flowers and pods. Other legumes, sweet peas for example, can be potentially harmful if eaten.

**Peas and French beans** are self-fertile and need no pollinators, while broad beans are best with pollinators but have sufficient self-pollination to get by without them. Runner beans are particular about their pollination requirements and often crop poorly if the flowers fail through drought or adverse weather or if bees bite the base of the flower to get the nectar without effecting pollination as they would via the normal route to the nectar. Modern cultivars include crosses with French beans that have resulted in a useful degree of self-pollination making the crop independent of pollinators and weather.

**Legumes** are grown from notably larger seeds than other vegetables, and produce large, fast-growing seedlings. Hardy legumes (broad beans and peas) can be sown quite early even outdoors and therefore crop in early summer when fresh produce is in short supply. Indeed the hardiest broad beans and peas can even be sown in autumn for especially early cropping the following summer. French and runner beans are tender and are sown indoors in mid-spring and outdoors in late spring.

**Climbing** French and runner beans are grown up wigwams or hedges of long canes or sticks, while peas are supported by twiggy sticks from hazel or, birch trees or more conveniently, wire mesh. Broad beans can be dwarf and require no support but stakes and string are often needed to prevent the plants falling under the weight of crop, or 'lodge', as this is known.

**Peas** come in two forms – those where the pods are edible and the more traditional type where only the seeds (peas) are eaten. The latter includes petit pois varieties with very small peas, of which you will need a fair number of plants to provide sufficient for your plate.

**Edible-podded** peas include the flatter podded mangetout types and the fatter podded cultivars often referred to by the name of an early cultivar, sugar pods. As they account for more food on your plate than shelled peas you will not need to sow as many.

**Pods** are usually green but purple-podded cultivars are offered. They make ornamental plants and in the case of edible-podded ones add colour to salads if lightly microwaved to avoid loss of pigment.

A wide range of **heights** can be grown – taller peas need supports but shorter ones need little or even no support. The shorter ones can be sown closer, so they generally out-yield the taller cultivars.

**Broad beans** may have red, white or white and black flowers. Red flowers lead to reddish pods and seeds, both ornamental. White flowers have low-tannin easily digested seeds.

**French beans** have amazingly diverse dry seeds and the edible pods can be yellow, red, purple or green or indeed streaked and speckled with these colours. Some cultivars are offered to grow dry beans such as borlotti, but a cool wet autumn can make gathering a sound crop difficult. Freezing semi-ripe beans is a very good alternative to drying.

# Tender vegetables

Cucumber family plants include courgettes, cucumbers, melons (traditionally considered under fruit), squash, pumpkin, vegetable marrows, potato family crops, aubergines, chilli and sweet peppers, tomatillo and sweetcorn. They are damaged or killed by even light frosts.

Similarly, **tender curiosities** such as oca and yacon, edible roots with an unusual flavour yet to achieve widespread acceptance, must be grown frost-free.

In all but **mild regions** these crops are started indoors in pots and planted out once the risk of frost has passed. Potato family crops have small seeds and are sown in early spring so the young plants can be big enough to plant out by early summer.

Cucumber family plants and **sweetcorn** have big seeds producing big seedlings and can be sown in mid-spring or even outdoors in late spring.

**Tender plants** have a lot of growing to do to mature in short summers. Adding rotted organic matter such as manure or garden compost prior to planting and also including a base dressing of fertilizer is wise; watering every 10–14 days in dry spells is also advisable.

Some **crops are gathered** as soon as they are big enough, for example courgettes, cucumbers and summer squash. Others are gathered when properly coloured, such as chilli and sweet peppers.

**Pumpkins**, winter squash and vegetable marrows for storing are cut with a short stalk as soon as the stalk dries up, the fruits ring hollow if lightly tapped, and the full expected colour has been reached.

**Unusually** for a vegetable, Sweetcorn is wind pollinated, and is usually grown in squares allowing about 50cm/20in between plants in all directions.

**Cucumber family plants** are big and are widely spaced; courgettes and cucumbers can be no closer than 50cm/20in with 1.2m/4ft between rows.

**Watering is advisable,** not least because it will help prevent powdery mildew disease for which no fungicides are offered, although tolerant cultivars are available.

Many **cucumber family plants** climb and can be grown up fences, arches and wigwams; climbing courgettes, cucumbers, trailing marrows, pumpkins and squash.

**Greenfly and caterpillars** can be troublesome, but tender plants are usually almost trouble-free.

# Tomatoes and potatoes

Tomatoes and potatoes are very closely related but potatoes are potentially harmful, except for their tubers of course. It is unwise to consume potato fruits or indeed any part of the plant save the tubers.

Any fertile, well-drained garden soil in full sun suits potatoes and tomatoes. Adding rotted manure or other organic matter and a base dressing of fertilizer about two weeks before planting is good practice. Both need plenty of potassium so a potassium-rich fertilizer is often a good choice.

Both are tender but potatoes can be planted as 'seed tubers' from early spring. Protection from frosts by earthing up – that is gathering soil over the emerging delicate shoots – or covering with paper or horticultural fleece will save the crop if untimely frosts threaten. As the crop grows, more and more soil is drawn up around the stems until the foliage meets in the middle of the rows. This is to exclude light that might turn the tubers green and inedible.

Tomatoes are thinly sown from late winter until early spring. Water to keep plants moist but never soggy. Seedlings are pricked-out into separate pots as soon as they can be handled. They need bright light, a windowsill or similar warm bright place. Give them more space as they grow – their leaves should never touch. Feed every week with liquid fertilizer from six weeks after potting or sooner if plants become pale.

Seed tubers are planted in rows 75cm/ 30in apart, 60cm/24in for earlies with about 30cm/12in between plants, 20cm/8in for earlies and with about 5–8cm/2–3in of soil over the tuber.

The warmer and **brighter** the site the more and better the tomatoes. Warm urban heat islands and sheltered south-facing gardens elsewhere are ideal.

Bush tomatoes need no pruning and are merely grown on black plastic mulch to keep the fruits clean, as the plants usually flop under the weight of the crop.

Potato blight is the bane of potatoes and tomatoes and in the absence of fungicides crops must be gathered early when disease is seen.

Salad potatoes produce smallish tubers, with delicate flavour and high dry matter which remain firm when cooked. They are ideal for salads and recipes that require firm-textured potatoes.

Bush tomatoes have a growing tip on the end of every shoot and flowers are borne on the stem.

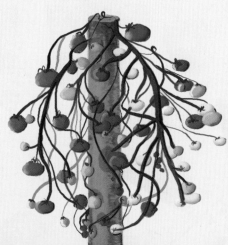

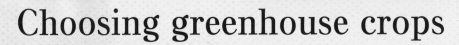

# Choosing greenhouse crops

Greenhouse space, whether glasshouse or plastic, is expensive and limited.
However, even a small area of protected cultivation can be highly productive.

**Summer crops** – aubergines, chilli and sweet peppers, cucumbers, melons and tomatoes – are the most important when the extra warmth and protection transforms tender summer crop – growing from an uncertain enterprise with limited and late harvests to one where good crops are almost certain.

There are **three sorts** of summer crops: cucumbers – which need lower light levels and higher humidity than other crops, tomatoes and melons which do well in high light and lowish humidity, and the remaining rather more tolerant crops that can put up with either extreme – which notably includes peppers.

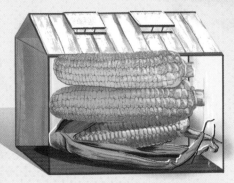

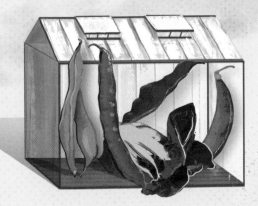

In **colder regions** sweetcorn is often only feasible in a greenhouse.

Summer crops are **cleared** by **autumn** when lower temperatures and light levels greatly limit what can be grown. Calabrese, French beans and Chinese mustard greens sown in late summer can crop well until late autumn.

**Salad crops,** particularly endive and lettuce sown in late summer are successful until deep winter. Some lettuces can grow heads in the short days of winter but usually the heater will be needed in severe cold spells or to dry out the foliage to prevent disease.

**Greenhouses get too hot** in summer and require good ventilation and shading. Blinds are best for shade but special white shade painting is widely used on glasshouses or shade netting draped over plastic greenhouses.

**Greenhouse tomatoes:** Set out plants 45cm/18in apart with the top of the pot level with the compost or soil. Water thoroughly and keep the rootball moist until the roots explore the surrounding compost.

**Pots and growing bags** must not be allowed to dry out. Keep them moist but never allow them to become saturated. Apply tomato fertilizer every week from 30 days after planting.

Tomato **flowers** usually set easily in home greenhouses, but in dull weather tapping the canes on sunny days helps the pollen move from male to female parts of the flower.

# Medicinal planting

Needless to say, medical advice should be sought for any significant health concern, and use of medicinal herbs should be discussed in advance with the relevant physician as herbal remedies could adversely interact with medication. However, garden remedies are usually a safe and natural addition to the first aid box and medicine cupboard.

Making herbal remedies is a specialist process and guidance should be sought on how to make and use the decoctions, juices, lotions, poultices, oils and teas. Happily the following plants are straightforward to grow.

Cinquefoil (*Potentilla reptans*), a wild perennial plant, can be a rather pernicious weed, but this also means it is easy to grow. The juice or infusion of the foliage or roots can be used to alleviate muscle spasms and fever and reduce the pain of ulcers and joints.

Roman or lawn camomile (*Anthemis nobilis*) is an ancient herbal remedy for digestive problems, breathing difficulties and pain. It is used as a tea made from the flowers or a lotion for external use.

## Scented

mayweed or German camomile (*Matricaria recutita*) a farm weed, is also used as tea or infused in oil for topical use to soothe burns, pains and wounds.

## Cultivated

liquorice (*Glycyrrhiza glabra*) is a traditional garden herb. It is perennial and grown for its roots which are used to make a tea effective against inflammation, muscle spasms, respiratory tract problems, urinary tract infections and digestive tract problems.

**Vervain** (*Verbena officinalis*) is an easily grown medium-sized perennial. Teas and concoctions made from the dried leaves, gathered just before flowering, are used to treat bruises, wounds, strains and every sort of pain and inflammation.

**Primroses** (*Primula vulgaris*), which are hardy perennials, have medicinal properties in addition to their ornamental value. An infusion of flowers and leaves can be used for fever, inflammation and pain relief.

# Choosing herbs

**Herbs** are easy to grow and take up little space. A good supply can come from a window box if need be. Most herbs require full sun, good drainage and shelter, but moderate fertility.

To make best use of **fresh herbs** they should ideally be near the back door and easily accessible from all weather paths. Growing through gravel reduces weeding and also protects the foliage from soil splash in heavy rain.

**Coriander, parsley and dill** are examples of the many that can be raised from seed either sown where they are to grow or in cell trays indoors. Sowing every few weeks ensures an uninterrupted supply of herbs in perfect condition.

**Bay, sage and thyme** are among the perennial herbs. They are usually best bought as plants or raised from cuttings in late summer.

**Watering** and feeding should be kept to the minimum for the best-flavoured herbs, but some, coriander and dill for example, may prematurely flower and set seed if stressed. Here watering is advisable.

Herbs are largely **free of pests** and diseases. Soap, fatty acid or oil-based insecticides will leave no residues on the herbs. Diseased materials should be removed when seen.

**Chives and mint** can be grown by dividing older plants and planting the young offsets for a new crop.

**Fennel** (*Foeniculum vulgare*) is a hardy perennial grown from seed, usually sown afresh every year.

**French tarragon** (*Artemisia dracunculus*) is a tender perennial. It needs fertile soil, warmth and good light.

**Rosemary** (*Rosmarinus officinalis*) is a fairly hardy evergreen shrub that requires well-drained soil in a sunny spot.

# Gathering and using herbs

Plants derive their flavour from the need to defend themselves. Imagine Mediterranean hillsides populated by goats. Herbs often have to survive frequent and heavy grazing and those such as bay, hyssop, lavender, marjoram, rosemary, sage and thyme are amenable to frequent cutting of young foliage. Constant cutting leads to healthier and longer-lived herbs. But it is unwise to take more than a third of the plant or to cut into older woody stems as recovery cannot be guaranteed. Using secateurs, a sharp knife, 'snips' or scissors gather 5–10cm/2–4in stems, ideally, for the best flavour, on a warm, still, sunny day and just prior to flowering. It is pleasing to cut so as to leave the plant with a balanced shape. Avoid mixing different herbs as you will lose the individual flavours and scents.

**Short-lived herbs** such as chervil, coriander, dill and parsley can be cut with relative abandon because they soon go over-mature, and in well-planned gardens follow-on sowings are growing to take their place. It is possible to harvest half the foliage and the plants will still recover to yield more before running to seed.

Although it is **fresh herbs** that really benefit from being home grown, surplus herbs can be dried. Dry herbs either in trays or in small bunches strung from strings.

**Once dried,** store herbs in airtight containers in the dark and check for mould from time to time, discarding any mouldy material.

If herbs are being **grown for seeds,** such as caraway, coriander, cumin, fennel or even mustard, the plants are supported so the seedheads are kept free of soil and rotting, and the heads cut as soon as the first seed falls. They can ripen indoors in seed trays lined with paper and when dry the seeds are separated from the other debris by sieving, winnowing (blowing) and hand picking. They are then stored cool and dry in sealed containers.

**Don't gather herbs** if you are unsure of the plants' identity.

**Microwave ovens** can be used to dry herbs when time is short, although excessive drying is significant risk.

Basil, mint and tarragon can be **preserved in vinegar.**

# Fruit
# & Vines

# Site and space

Fruit trees and bushes are one of the more expensive investments when planting a garden, so it makes sense to give them the best site available, and to invest also in shelter and protection from birds, which can quickly strip a crop of ripening fruit.

Ideally **keep** the **soil** around apple trees free of vegetation, or if grassed keep it mown short. This creates a reserve of warmth in the soil that is radiated out at night, protecting the trees.

**Particularly** in a garden situation, frost protection can be given to bushes and small trees by covering them with horticultural fleece or old curtains.

In **very small gardens** much use can be made of walls and fences to grow climbing hybrid berries such as loganberries, grapevines or, in warm regions, kiwi fruit. Arches and pillars are also useful supports.

**Raspberries** are the most productive fruit crop and the best investment where space is limited.

Where the **aspect** is not perfect, cooking cultivars of apples, sour cherries and, to a lesser extent pears and plums are more tolerant of adverse conditions than the finest dessert cultivars.

Almost any **well-drained** garden soil will grow successful fruit trees and bushes.

**Grouping** all the **fruit** in a small plot allows you to protect it with a fruit cage and eases the other tasks of maintenance, such as spraying and feeding.

**Full sun** is best for fruit but in many cases this is just not possible, so in a cold situation stick to early ripening apples, pears and plums, as well as raspberries and gooseberries.

**Strawberries** can be grown in the vegetable garden and make a useful break in a three-year rotation system.

# Choosing

There has seldom been such a wide range of fruit offered as you can find today and as few people can fit more than a limited number of plants into their garden it is necessary to be selective.

Another consideration is that trees are **expensive** and slow-growing. Maiden or one-year-old trees are the cheapest option, but the buyer has to do all the formative training themselves. So if this does not appeal to you, then ready-trained trees, several years old, are a more suitable choice.

Many **less usual cultivars** are propagated to order, so may take two years or more until they are ready to be delivered and planted.

**Soft fruits** include raspberries, blackberries, blueberries, loganberries, Japanese wineberries and strawberries.

**Acid soils** are required for cranberries and blueberries, but in gardens where this cannot be provided, they also grow well in containers of acid (ericaceous) potting medium.

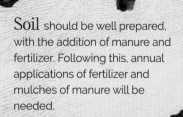

Soil should be well prepared, with the addition of manure and fertilizer. Following this, annual applications of fertilizer and mulches of manure will be needed.

Soft fruits produce a very high yield for the area of ground used.

Soft fruits often lend themselves to **container cultivation** on patios.

Soft fruits crop over a **long season**, with strawberries from late spring and raspberries into mid-autumn.

Soft fruits **do not** store well and have to be used fresh, frozen or preserved.

Prune soft fruits every year for good results.

Tree fruits include apples, gages, medlars, mulberries, pears, plums, quinces, sweet cherries and sour cherries. These can be grown in restricted or bush forms but usually need more space than soft fruit.

Tree height is dictated by rootstocks that can either dwarf trees or promote the vigorous, tall growth needed for specimen trees.

Unlike soft fruits, trees should not be planted into very fertile soil as this encourages excess growth and delayed flowering after planting.

# Rootstocks

Rootstocks are a fundamental part of growing the desired tree. In particular, a rootstock can reduce vigour and increase fruitfulness to ensure a manageable trees for small spaces. Many space-saving tree forms such as cordons would be impossible without dwarfing rootstocks that limit the tree's ultimate size while retaining productivity.

**Fruit trees** seldom grow as successfully on their own roots as they do on a carefully selected rootstock – they may not root well, they may get too big or fail to crop well.

Fruit trees are almost always created by joining a shoot to a root. The shoot (or scion) is a cultivar with useful properties, such as apple 'Gala', while the rootstock governs the tree's size and often confers protection against disease.

The **join** or **graft** is made by an exact cut to behead the rootstock and to shape the shoot so their living tissues match and fuse to make a new tree.

Not **every combination** is successful, and in a few cases graft incompatibility can occur unless an 'interstock' of a different tree compatible with both rootstock and scion is grafted in as a go-between, an extra complexity that raises the cost of the tree.

Weaker-growing **rootstocks** have less vigorous roots and usually require staking all their lives.

The **bigger** the **tree** the more room it requires. When buying a fruit tree it is wise to get one on a rootstock whose expected ultimate size is consistent with the available space.

An excessively **vigorous** rootstock may lead to a tree that needs so much pruning to keep it within bounds that cropping is impaired.

**Rootstocks** can also make up for poor soil. Thin, dry and infertile soil calls for a more vigorous rootstock, so a semi-dwarfing stock would be used in place of a fully dwarfing one.

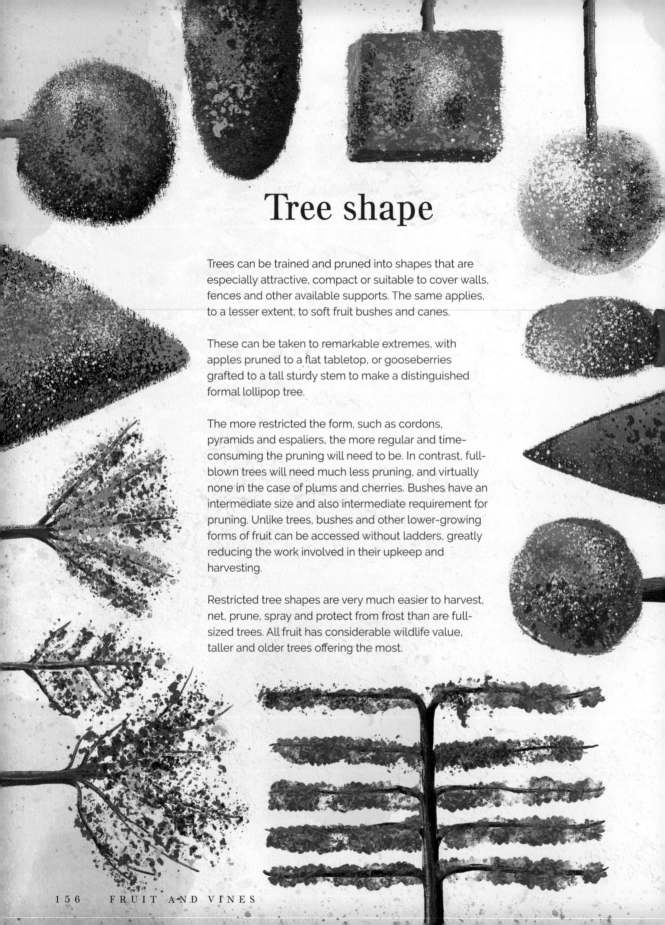

# Tree shape

Trees can be trained and pruned into shapes that are especially attractive, compact or suitable to cover walls, fences and other available supports. The same applies, to a lesser extent, to soft fruit bushes and canes.

These can be taken to remarkable extremes, with apples pruned to a flat tabletop, or gooseberries grafted to a tall sturdy stem to make a distinguished formal lollipop tree.

The more restricted the form, such as cordons, pyramids and espaliers, the more regular and time-consuming the pruning will need to be. In contrast, full-blown trees will need much less pruning, and virtually none in the case of plums and cherries. Bushes have an intermediate size and also intermediate requirement for pruning. Unlike trees, bushes and other lower-growing forms of fruit can be accessed without ladders, greatly reducing the work involved in their upkeep and harvesting.

Restricted tree shapes are very much easier to harvest, net, prune, spray and protect from frost than are full-sized trees. All fruit has considerable wildlife value, taller and older trees offering the most.

Cordons are the most useful tree shape, being just a single stem. Cordons can be vertical but are easier to control when grown at about 45 degrees, the angled stem inhibiting growth and promoting fruitfulness.

Step-over apples are horizontal cordons of very low vigour, used to edge kitchen garden plots. They must have a very dwarfing rootstock to be feasible, and such rootstocks are only offered for apples.

Like cordons, bush trees, pyramids and spindlebushes can be grown with a central stem, with fruiting branches radiating out. Pyramids are summer pruned to keep the trees fruitful and to size, but spindlebushes rely on heavily cropping lower branches tied down to near-horizontal to limit size.

Fans and espaliers involve training the shoots up walls and fences either in spreading form or with ladder-like side branches. This makes good use of walls and fences, being very space-efficient.

Palmettes are essentially several cordons on a single tree, trained into a hand-like pattern. The bends involved in making the cordons and the horizontal stems from which they arise greatly reduce the vigour in these highly ornamental tree forms.

Bushes are trained to a goblet, open-centred shape and are the easiest form to maintain, but even with dwarfing rootstocks take more space than highly restrained forms.

Trees are best reserved for ornament or cider orchards, as they are just too big for gardens and need ladders for picking and pruning.

# Planting

Fruit bushes are expected to last 10–15 years and fruit trees 30 years or more, so it makes sense, and indeed is essential, to choose the most appropriate cultivars grown on suitable rootstocks, and then to plant well to ensure that they get away to a good start.

Unfortunately it is easy to plant too deeply as container-grown plants are often potted mechanically and set in their pots on the deep side in the nursery. This can mislead gardeners into planting out at the wrong level. It is good practice with container plants to remove surplus potting medium until the 'flare' of the roots can be found, and then plant so the roots are only just below soil level.

Waterlogged soil is a common cause of failure. Where the ground tends to lie wet, planting on a slight mound of 25cm/10in can keep the base of plants free from excess water. Soil preparation should be done in advance of planting.

Bare-root plants are especially economical, but if the ground is not in a fit state to receive them they must be temporarily planted in a spare piece of ground to protect the roots from freezing and drying. This process is called 'heeling in'.

Watering in the first summer after planting, and perhaps also in the second, is crucial for survival.

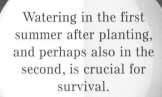

**Container-grown** fruit can be planted at any time, although the dormant period is best.

As **fruit trees** and **bushes** are in place for some years, a soil analysis followed by feeding, liming and manuring to address any deficiency is a good investment.

Trees will often **need** a **stake**, and this is best hammered in before planting the tree but after digging the hole.

The planting hole should be just deep enough that the roots are covered with soil and no more.

**After planting** it is good practice to apply a mulch around, but not touching, the base of the tree.

# Training

Training covers the first few years of a tree's life, much of it in the fruit nursery getting the tree into a good shape for sale. Cordons need little training, as they are grown on a single stem, while espaliers are built up in tiers and require several years of painstaking tying in and pruning.

Without **careful training** trees develop adverse shapes that do not intercept light efficiently, provide harbourage for diseases and pests, and are prone to breakage from premature cropping on weak branches.

On the other hand, **excessively severe** formative pruning can result in rampant growth that is too leafy and vigorous to form flower buds, which consequently delays flowering and fruit production.

**Soft fruits** need much less training than fruit trees. Blackcurrants are merely cut to ground level after planting. Gooseberries, and white and redcurrants, are grown on a little trunk called a 'leg'.

Exceptions are standard or lollipop-style gooseberries and currants, which need reasonably skilful training to get a pleasing and productive shape.

**Maiden** and other young trees establish best. However, maiden fruit trees will need several years of training in many cases.

Many **fan-trained trees** are sold with a central stem in addition to angled stems. Ideally, however, these need careful removal of the central stem to create a shapely fan.

**Espaliers** have to be made rung by rung, with one new level each year. Attempts to make several rungs at once are seldom satisfactory.

# Pruning

After the training period, fruit trees and bushes are pruned to enhance cropping and to contain size. Plants have a natural propensity to fruit and crop, but the heaviest and most regular crops are achieved if the tree is pruned to shift its activities towards flowering and fruit production.

This is achieved by manipulating the balance between mature fruiting wood and younger, more vigorous but less fruitful wood. As older wood gets increasingly unproductive with age this is also judiciously removed.

Bear in mind when pruning that the amount of fruit produced affects the growth of new shoots. If there are heavy crops of fruit the new shoots required to replace older shoots will not make adequate growth.

Prunings must be disposed of either by burning or by shredding in order to speed up the rotting process. The wood can support diseases such as the fungal silver leaf disease that can infect fruit trees and cause severe damage.

**Winter pruning** removes dormant wood, and as the plant stores its food reserves in the roots, the result is vigorous growth in spring. So while it may sometimes appear that winter pruning makes trees bigger, this is in fact not the case.

**Summer pruning** removes leaves and also food reserves, and the tree cannot respond in the same way as it does to winter pruning. Summer pruning greatly weakens trees.

**Renewal pruning** is practised where a few whole branches are removed each year and new replacement branches selected. This is generally done with a pruning saw and is the pruning method of choice for larger trees.

Modern pruning saws are accurate, fast and do little damage, and are the preferred pruning tool for any wood that is too thick to be dealt with by secateurs. Loppers are much less satisfactory. Anvil secateurs are inferior to bypass ones.

**Hygiene** involves cleaning tools after use on each tree, by wiping them using a cloth soaked in garden disinfectant.

# Apples and pears

Despite the widespread availability of very dwarfing rootstocks many excessively large and hard-to-maintain apple trees remain, largely due to the misguided selling of trees on the over-vigorous MM106 rootstock. Having said that, where there is space these larger trees are very beneficial to wildlife.

Apples and pears are **highly dependent** on good pollination, and adverse spring weather can inhibit pollinating insects. Shelter from winds will help to provide favourable conditions. However, apples and pears are rarely self-fertile and need pollen from another, different cultivar to set fruit.

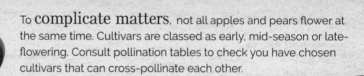

To **complicate matters**, not all apples and pears flower at the same time. Cultivars are classed as early, mid-season or late-flowering. Consult pollination tables to check you have chosen cultivars that can cross-pollinate each other.

Apples are ready to gather when the first fruits begin to fall. Early cultivars remain sound for only a brief period, so care should be taken not to grow too many.

Modern **tastes** for apples tend towards the crunchy, sweet and juicy cultivars like 'Braeburn'. In areas where this variety does not do well, others, such as 'Fuji', 'Gala', 'Greensleeves' and 'Scrumptious' can fill in.

Even after fruit has set **problems remain**, as excess fruit can break branches and reduce the tree's cropping capacity for the following year. To avoid this, carry out thinning by removing a proportion of the fruit in midsummer.

Pears are **somewhat trickier** than apples to harvest as once they begin to fall they tend to be over-ripe and squidgy inside. A better method is to bite into them as they assume their ripe colour and once they taste sweet, gather and ripen them in a cool place indoors.

**Good pears** include 'Beth' (early), 'Beurré Hardy' (mid-season) and 'Concorde' (later).

# Blueberries

Blueberries have large bright indigo berries in summer and early autumn. They were developed in the USA and botanically they are a form of *Vaccinium* (*V. corymbosum* – 'high bush' attaining up to 2m/6½ft, *V. angustifolium* – 'low bush', and hybrids of the two species of intermediate height 50–120cm/20–48in known as 'half high').

These **hardy deciduous shrubs** are highly intolerant of alkaline soils and need plenty of space. Allow high bush cultivars at least 1–1.5m/3¼–5ft and half-high cultivars 1m/3¼ft between plants. High bush cultivars are the most widely grown.

They are **bought** as **bushes** and ideally planted in autumn, but can be planted at all seasons if pot-raised. They thrive in pots of ericaceous growing medium and ideally are watered with rainwater. Peat-free ericaceous potting media are now available and to be preferred. Pots are much the best option when the garden soil is alkaline or heavy clay. Another alternative is to make raised beds of acid or acidified soil. As ericaceous media tend to be rather fine-textured and prone to wetness and resultant root diseases, it is advisable to repot blueberries every two years into fresh compost, discarding about 30 per cent of the older roots and adjacent medium.

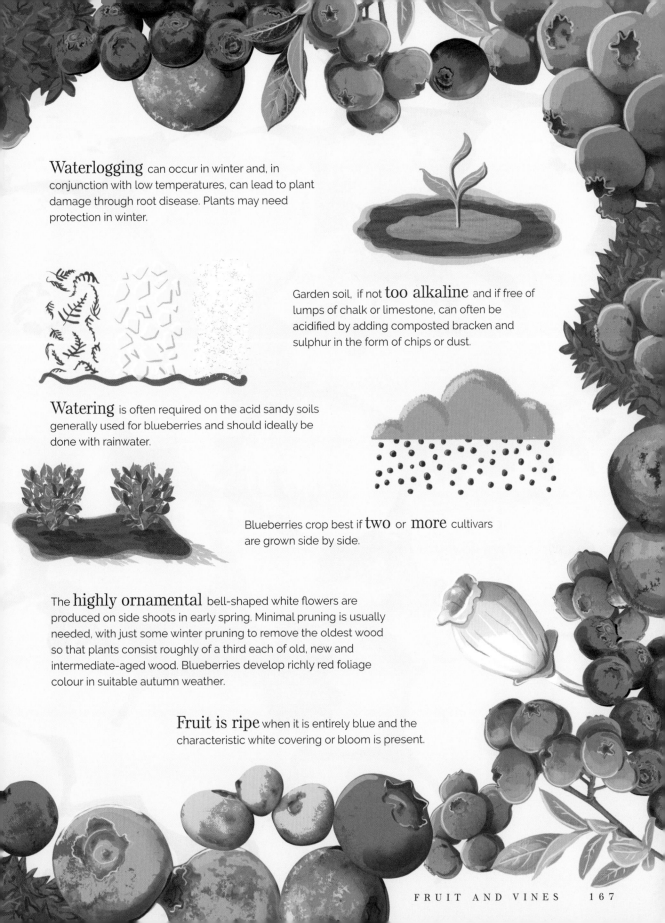

**Waterlogging** can occur in winter and, in conjunction with low temperatures, can lead to plant damage through root disease. Plants may need protection in winter.

Garden soil, if not **too alkaline** and if free of lumps of chalk or limestone, can often be acidified by adding composted bracken and sulphur in the form of chips or dust.

**Watering** is often required on the acid sandy soils generally used for blueberries and should ideally be done with rainwater.

Blueberries crop best if **two** or **more** cultivars are grown side by side.

The **highly ornamental** bell-shaped white flowers are produced on side shoots in early spring. Minimal pruning is usually needed, with just some winter pruning to remove the oldest wood so that plants consist roughly of a third each of old, new and intermediate-aged wood. Blueberries develop richly red foliage colour in suitable autumn weather.

**Fruit is ripe** when it is entirely blue and the characteristic white covering or bloom is present.

# Strawberries

Modern **high-yielding** disease-resistant strawberries lend themselves to smaller gardens, where they can be covered in cloches or fleece to produce early crops.

**June-fruiting** cultivars are the next to crop, while new everbearing and day-neutral strawberries offer lighter but prolonged cropping into the autumn.

Strawberries are **not fussy** and any well-drained, reasonably fertile garden soil will suit them. However good light is required, as well as shelter.

**Frosts** can give them a severe nip as they are low-growing (and thus vulnerable to cold air, which accumulates at ground level), and also flower early.

It is very **difficult to weed** strawberries, so areas where they are to be planted should be free of perennial weeds such as bindweed and couch grass.

If strawberries are to be **grown** in the vegetable garden, which is a good idea, they should not follow potatoes as spuds transmit the fungal disease verticillium wilt, to which strawberries are very prone.

**Planting** is ideally done in early autumn for best results in the following year, but in practice plants are often only available at a later date.

Plants **set out in spring** are best not allowed to crop in the first year. Each plantation will last up to four years.

**Generous spacing** (45cm/18in) is wise with strawberries, as congested plants produce small fruits and can be severely diseased.

By **picking** every two or three days, perfectly ripe soft, aromatic fruit can be gathered for immediate consumption. For jam-making the fruits are gathered firmer but still ripe.

When **June-bearers** crop, each cultivar produces for about two weeks. These include 'Honeoye', 'Hapil' and 'Red Gauntlet' – for mid-season and late 'Florence' and 'Symphony'.

**Everbearers** such as 'Calypso' and 'Buddy' crop at intervals through the growing season, usually in spring and autumn, producing relatively small fruits.

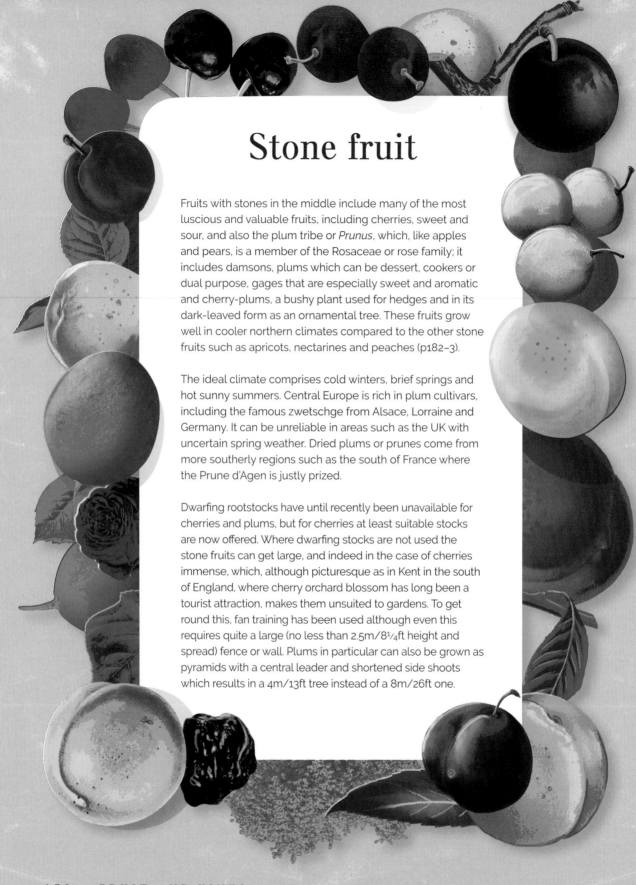

# Stone fruit

Fruits with stones in the middle include many of the most luscious and valuable fruits, including cherries, sweet and sour, and also the plum tribe or *Prunus*, which, like apples and pears, is a member of the Rosaceae or rose family; it includes damsons, plums which can be dessert, cookers or dual purpose, gages that are especially sweet and aromatic and cherry-plums, a bushy plant used for hedges and in its dark-leaved form as an ornamental tree. These fruits grow well in cooler northern climates compared to the other stone fruits such as apricots, nectarines and peaches (p182–3).

The ideal climate comprises cold winters, brief springs and hot sunny summers. Central Europe is rich in plum cultivars, including the famous zwetschge from Alsace, Lorraine and Germany. It can be unreliable in areas such as the UK with uncertain spring weather. Dried plums or prunes come from more southerly regions such as the south of France where the Prune d'Agen is justly prized.

Dwarfing rootstocks have until recently been unavailable for cherries and plums, but for cherries at least suitable stocks are now offered. Where dwarfing stocks are not used the stone fruits can get large, and indeed in the case of cherries immense, which, although picturesque as in Kent in the south of England, where cherry orchard blossom has long been a tourist attraction, makes them unsuited to gardens. To get round this, fan training has been used although even this requires quite a large (no less than 2.5m/8¼ft height and spread) fence or wall. Plums in particular can also be grown as pyramids with a central leader and shortened side shoots which results in a 4m/13ft tree instead of a 8m/26ft one.

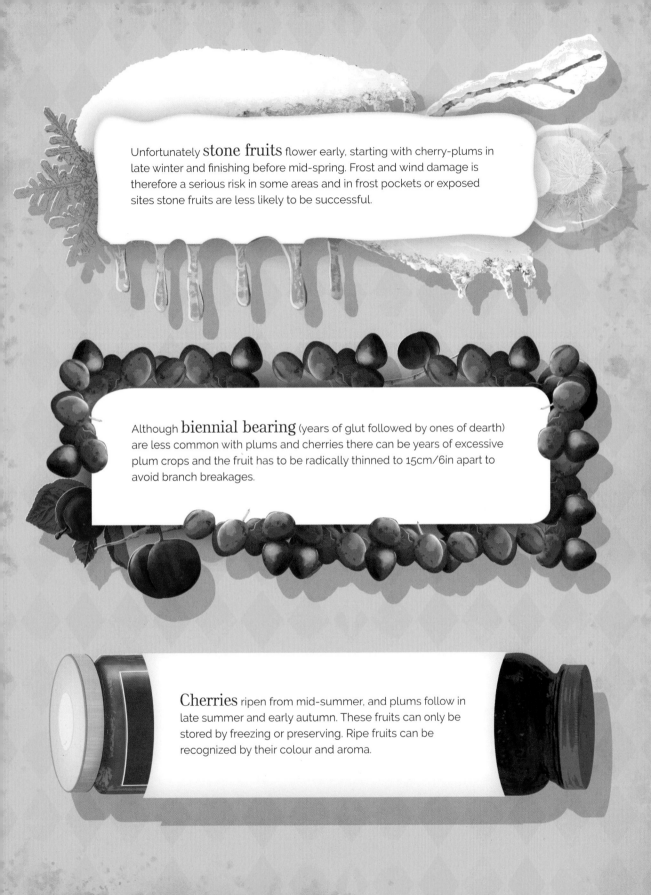

Unfortunately **stone fruits** flower early, starting with cherry-plums in late winter and finishing before mid-spring. Frost and wind damage is therefore a serious risk in some areas and in frost pockets or exposed sites stone fruits are less likely to be successful.

Although **biennial bearing** (years of glut followed by ones of dearth) are less common with plums and cherries there can be years of excessive plum crops and the fruit has to be radically thinned to 15cm/6in apart to avoid branch breakages.

**Cherries** ripen from mid-summer, and plums follow in late summer and early autumn. These fruits can only be stored by freezing or preserving. Ripe fruits can be recognized by their colour and aroma.

# Figs

Figs are a very valuable and easily grown garden crop. They are an ancient crop cultivated for thousands of years in the eastern Mediterranean. Their origin means they are well adapted to sweat out hot summers and survive mild wet winters. Although by nature a large tree, they respond very well to pruning which in combination with restriction of the root zone keeps them small and productive so that even a small garden can accommodate a fig.

**Observant gardeners** will see that they have no flowers – indeed a Chinese name for fig means 'fruit with no flower'. This is because the fruits actually contain the flowers on the inside, and in the wild pollination is effected by a tiny wasp that enters the flower through a convenient pore, and moves round it laying eggs and fertilizing the fruits, a process referred to as caprification. For this reason figs in hot countries often have a wasp larvae inside.

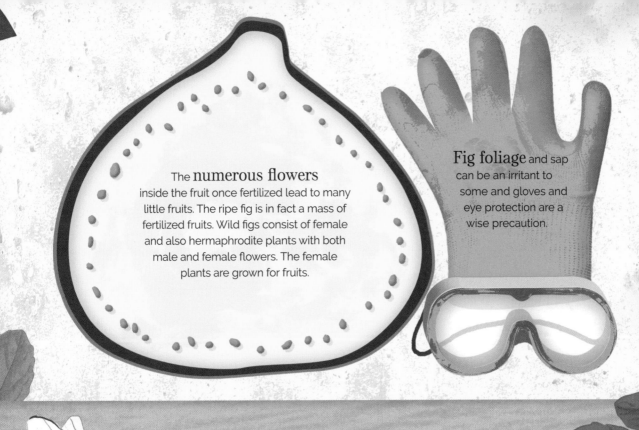

The **numerous flowers** inside the fruit once fertilized lead to many little fruits. The ripe fig is in fact a mass of fertilized fruits. Wild figs consist of female and also hermaphrodite plants with both male and female flowers. The female plants are grown for fruits.

**Fig foliage** and sap can be an irritant to some and gloves and eye protection are a wise precaution.

Unfortunately the **caprifying wasp** only lives in hot countries. However, figs that set fruit without pollination (parthenocarpic) have been developed and can therefore be grown in northerly regions. Although the flavour of self-fertile figs is considered to be inferior to the caprified or Smyrna fig they are still delicious.

**Figs are sensitive** to cold and won't survive prolonged freezing weather. Cultivars of figs for northern regions are notably hardier than southern figs, but cannot be considered to be reliably hardy.

**Fruit** is gathered as it becomes soft and sweetly scented. Figs cannot be stored although in hot regions many are dried. Fig preserves are probably more practical in colder climates.

**Figs are easily grown** in 45–60cm/18–24in diameter pots filled with John Innes No.2 soil-based growing media.

# Vine fruit

**Climbing fruits** are restricted to grapevines and kiwi fruits, both of which are deciduous. Both greatly benefit from a warming climate and are likely to figure more in northern gardens in the future.

**Grapes** are hardy perennial woody climbing shrubs that have been cultivated from ancient times. They are thought to have originated in central Asia, but the main cultivation regions have a Mediterranean climate. This gives a clue to their needs – they are hardy in winter, but need much light and warmth to fruit. They flower in late spring and are vulnerable to frosts at this time and indeed the foliage can be badly scorched by frost in mid-spring. Flowering late, they also fruit late which is well enough in the hot, dry late summer climate of Mediterranean regions but in cooler, wetter northerly areas the grapes ripen in autumn when the weather can be dull and wet. Without sun and dry weather the fruits will be low in sugar and somewhat sour, while the berries will be vulnerable to disease.

**In gardens,** skilled positioning in sunny sheltered spots, ideally against walls, will greatly improve the quantity, quality and timeliness of crops. Grapes make an excellent greenhouse crop with succulent fruit that compares favourably with supermarket bunches. They are slightly tricky in pots but can be very effective.

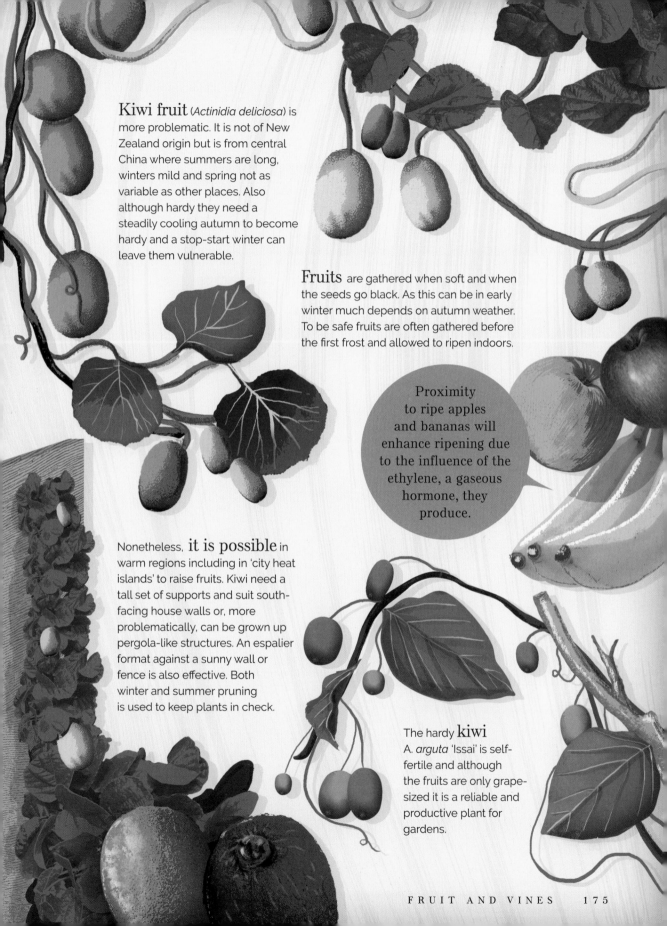

Kiwi fruit (*Actinidia deliciosa*) is more problematic. It is not of New Zealand origin but is from central China where summers are long, winters mild and spring not as variable as other places. Also although hardy they need a steadily cooling autumn to become hardy and a stop-start winter can leave them vulnerable.

Fruits are gathered when soft and when the seeds go black. As this can be in early winter much depends on autumn weather. To be safe fruits are often gathered before the first frost and allowed to ripen indoors.

Proximity to ripe apples and bananas will enhance ripening due to the influence of the ethylene, a gaseous hormone, they produce.

Nonetheless, it is possible in warm regions including in 'city heat islands' to raise fruits. Kiwi need a tall set of supports and suit south-facing house walls or, more problematically, can be grown up pergola-like structures. An espalier format against a sunny wall or fence is also effective. Both winter and summer pruning is used to keep plants in check.

The hardy kiwi A. *arguta* 'Issai' is self-fertile and although the fruits are only grape-sized it is a reliable and productive plant for gardens.

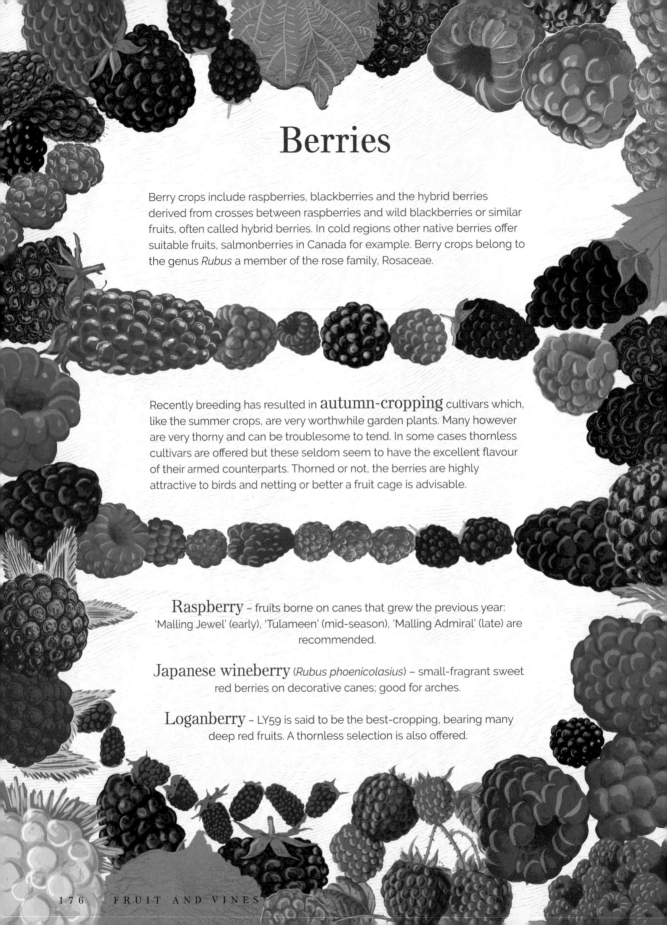

# Berries

Berry crops include raspberries, blackberries and the hybrid berries derived from crosses between raspberries and wild blackberries or similar fruits, often called hybrid berries. In cold regions other native berries offer suitable fruits, salmonberries in Canada for example. Berry crops belong to the genus *Rubus* a member of the rose family, Rosaceae.

Recently breeding has resulted in autumn-cropping cultivars which, like the summer crops, are very worthwhile garden plants. Many however are very thorny and can be troublesome to tend. In some cases thornless cultivars are offered but these seldom seem to have the excellent flavour of their armed counterparts. Thorned or not, the berries are highly attractive to birds and netting or better a fruit cage is advisable.

Raspberry – fruits borne on canes that grew the previous year: 'Malling Jewel' (early), 'Tulameen' (mid-season), 'Malling Admiral' (late) are recommended.

Japanese wineberry (*Rubus phoenicolasius*) – small-fragrant sweet red berries on decorative canes; good for arches.

Loganberry – LY59 is said to be the best-cropping, bearing many deep red fruits. A thornless selection is also offered.

Another name for berries is **cane fruit** as the plants are either upright canes as with raspberries or trailing stems as in blackberries and hybrid berries. In both cases wires tautly strung between posts are commonly used, but for effect canes can be trained over ornamental trellis and on arches. The canes typically grow one year and crop the following year. Therefore training involves presenting the canes from last year well tied in and convenient for controlling pests and diseases and gathering fruits, and to allow the new canes to form from ground level and spread with a minimum of hindrance. After cropping the spent fruited canes are cut out and the young canes tied in to crop the following year.

As **cropping** depends on producing abundant young canes each year feeding, manuring, mulching and watering in dry spells should be generous. A plantation of canes can be expected to last 9–12 years. However soil pests (nematodes or microscopic eelworms) and viruses spread by aphids and eelworms accumulate and plantations eventually decline in productivity. For some crops, especially raspberries, there are accreditation schemes that supply high health status plants to the market and every effort should be made to buy these.

**Boysenberry** – large black-red fruits on long canes.
A thornless selection is also offered.

**Tayberry** – large red fruits, heavy yielder.

**Blackberries** – cultivated ones include 'Loch Ness'
(compact but heavy-yielding) and 'Sylvan'
(vigorous and large fruits).

# Currants, gooseberries and allies

Currants, (*Ribes* spp) include black, pink, red and white currants, gooseberries and some less commonly grown and arguably undervalued relatives such as jostaberries and worcester berries.

They are not of ancient origin but have been cultivated in Europe for several hundred years. Their flavour is apt to be sharp or musky and not to everybody's taste; the majority of the commercial currant crop is processed into jam, jelly, juice and other products.

Currants do best in full light, but gooseberries will crop in light shade.

Any reasonable garden soil will support good crops of currants. Blackcurrants require higher fertility and are typically mulched with rotted organic matter, ideally manure, and receive nitrogen-rich general fertilizer in spring.

Gooseberries and red and other currants on the other hand crop on older wood and are not richly fed as this would induce productive timber and also leave the plants vulnerable to pests and disease.

Although **blackcurrants** are best grown as bushes other currants and gooseberries are readily grown against fences, wires and walls as cordons or fans, which, being quite small, are ideal for gardens. In fact gooseberry fans can be considered for east- and even north-facing sites.

## Plants last about 7–12 years until they get too large and woody, or until virus diseases accumulate. As new improved cultivars are often offered it is well worth replanting on a fresh piece of ground with the best available stock. Certified virus-free blackcurrant plants are available.

**Fruit** is gathered when coloured and soft although green gooseberries are better for jam-making. Redcurrants can be stored in the salad compartment of the refrigerator for many weeks but other currants can only be preserved or frozen. Unfortunately, unless plantations are netted birds are liable to take the crop.

## Pink currants, 1–1.5m/3¼–5ft; Gloire de Sablon – decorative as well as making pink jelly.

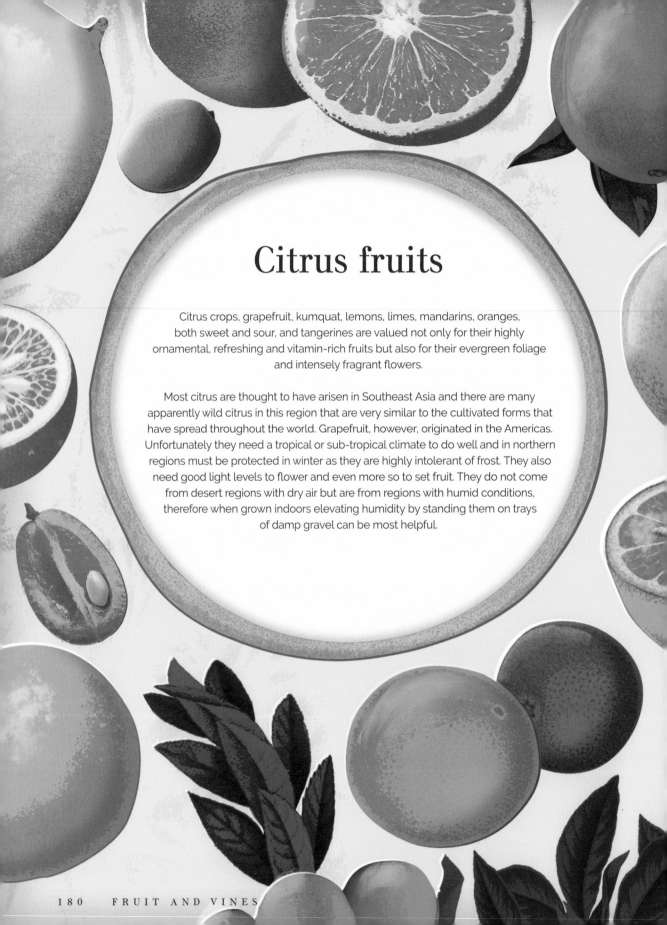

# Citrus fruits

Citrus crops, grapefruit, kumquat, lemons, limes, mandarins, oranges, both sweet and sour, and tangerines are valued not only for their highly ornamental, refreshing and vitamin-rich fruits but also for their evergreen foliage and intensely fragrant flowers.

Most citrus are thought to have arisen in Southeast Asia and there are many apparently wild citrus in this region that are very similar to the cultivated forms that have spread throughout the world. Grapefruit, however, originated in the Americas. Unfortunately they need a tropical or sub-tropical climate to do well and in northern regions must be protected in winter as they are highly intolerant of frost. They also need good light levels to flower and even more so to set fruit. They do not come from desert regions with dry air but are from regions with humid conditions, therefore when grown indoors elevating humidity by standing them on trays of damp gravel can be most helpful.

Although citrus can be grown indoors in greenhouses and conservatories or on windowsills their requirement for good light means they are exceptionally appreciative of being outdoors in a sunny spot during the summer.

Indoors high light levels are required and also moderate heat. They are easily harmed by the hot dry atmosphere of a centrally heated home and often do best on a sunny windowsill in an unheated room.

Citrus do best in an acidic potting medium (ericaceous) and one that is well fed in summer with nitrogen-rich fertilizers. In winter a balanced liquid feed can be used.

Citrus are easily raised from pips but these can take years before they flower and fruit. However, they are likely to be similar to their parents as citrus seeds are often 'apomictic' and arise solely from the parent without fertilization with pollen from another plant.

Little or no pruning is needed although, if needs be, plants will respond well to pruning in spring where required to restrict size or shape a plant.

# Apricots, nectarines and peaches

Like cherries and plums, apricots (*Prunus armeniaca*) and peaches (*P. persica*) are members of the Rosaceae family, but they need more warmth and are usually grown in more southerly regions, or, in Northern regions, in sheltered sunny areas. Nectarines are peaches that have smooth rather than furry skin.

**Peaches** and **apricots** originated in China in regions with short but cold winters and hot summers and where spring frosts are uncommon. Conditions in other words quite different from northern Europe. Nonetheless gardeners, by using ingenuity and care, can enjoy these fruits eaten as they should be – freshly picked, rather than after some days in a refrigerated lorry. Any good garden soil will support these trees.

**Although apricots,** peaches and nectarines grow and indeed usually crop if raised from seed, best results come from buying grafted plants. There are no dwarfing rootstocks but as well as the semi-vigorous plum rootstock 'St Julian A' some other plum rootstocks are semi-dwarfing and include Torinel and Montclare.

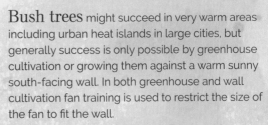

**Bush trees** might succeed in very warm areas including urban heat islands in large cities, but generally success is only possible by greenhouse cultivation or growing them against a warm sunny south-facing wall. In both greenhouse and wall cultivation fan training is used to restrict the size of the fan to fit the wall.

**It is difficult** to satisfactorily train these plants against small walls (less than 2m /6½ft). Patio peaches are often offered which are naturally very dwarf, need no pruning, suit small spaces and are very reliable.

**Peach leaf curl** is a destructive fungal disease that infects peaches and nectarines as well as rather less commonly apricots if the foliage is wet in late winter. Greenhouse cultivation avoids this and shelters can be made against walls to shed rain.

**As the flowering time** is early and pollinators may be scarce outdoors, or indeed absent when flowering under wall protection or in greenhouses, artificial pollination is often used. A soft paint brush can be used on sunny afternoons to shift pollen around the flowers. Several sessions may be required over the two weeks of flowering so that these trees fruit. As they are self-fertile there is no need to transfer pollen from plant to plant.

# Fruit in pots

Fruit is a long-term investment and people who anticipate moving home from time to time might wish to grow their fruit trees and bushes in a portable form in containers.

Others find their best sites in their gardens are too small to accommodate fully grown fruit trees and resort to containers. However, fruits in flower and crop are attractive in their own right and container-grown fruit are an asset to any patio. A useful side-effect of container fruit cultivation is the 'dwarfing effect' of pots on trees, making them not just somewhat smaller than their open-ground counterparts but also more fruitful. Although container-grown fruit is best pruned as recommended for the fruit in question, less pruning will be required.

The bigger the pot the easier to manage the tree or bush. On the other hand large containers are very hard to move. A minimum size of 45cm/18in diameter allows good portability and reasonably easy cultivation.

As with **all container plants** it is good practice to repot into a bigger pot or replace in the same pot after removing 25 per cent of roots and potting medium and replacing with fresh potting medium, every two or three years. In the intervening period replacing the top 5cm/2in of potting medium with fresh each year is very beneficial to the trees and bushes. Adding a resin-coated controlled-release fertilizer at this stage can feed the plant all season avoiding the need for frequent summer liquid feeding.

A soil-based **potting medium** such as John Innes No.3 is easiest to manage and being heavy offers good stability to taller plants. However, any coarse-textured growing medium should be satisfactory.

Good drainage is essential, but trees and large shrubs can quickly deplete water supplies in even large pots and an automatic watering system is well worth considering to protect what may be several years of growing and careful cultivation.

All these fruits can be left outdoors in winter.

Cherries      Pears      Apples      Plums      Olives

# Practicalities

# Lime and acidity

Soil can be acid, alkaline or neutral, and this is expressed by the pH scale. The lower the pH value the more acid, and the higher the more alkaline, with pH7 being neutral. The main influence on pH is the amount of calcium present. Acid soils have less calcium and alkaline ones more. The ideal pH for plant growth is pH6–6.5 or slightly acid, although ericaceous or lime-hating plants such as rhododendrons and many heathers prefer a pH of about 5.5.

In acid soils almost all trace elements are readily available, but so is aluminium. It is very damaging to plants and plant growth is often poor on acid soils due to aluminium toxicity.

5 pH     5.5 pH     6 pH

Excessively acid soils are easily treated with inexpensive lime to raise the pH. Lime can be ground limestone or chalk, hydrated lime from builders' suppliers or wood ash. Liming materials should be finely ground into dust, as lumpy lime takes many years to react. Sandy soils need much less lime than clay soils and guidance charts are supplied to calculate the amount of lime needed to raise the pH to 6.5 for different soil types. Sometimes to control clubroot disease of cabbages a higher pH of 7.5 is required and extra lime can be added to accomplish this.

Gardeners then need to know the pH of their soil. Often a look around can help. If neighbouring gardens are rich in camellias, heathers and rhododendrons, and if hydrangeas are blue-flowered, it is likely to be an acid soil area. Test kits are inexpensive and give a usefully accurate pH although a laboratory test is better.

High pH soils 'lock up' almost all trace elements (molybdenum is the exception), particularly iron. Ericaceous plants are much less able to acquire iron than other plants and typically develop yellow foliage (chlorosis) and fail to thrive in alkaline soils.

.5 pH

7 pH

8 pH

Lime takes several months to react and is best applied before planting and incorporated into the soil. If left on the surface it will take several years to raise the pH of the root zone. The action of rain and certain fertilizers lowers pH so repeated liming every five years is often required. Over-liming is common in gardens and care in application and measurement will avoid wasting lime and reducing plant health.

# Soil care

Traditionally soil has been dug every winter, turning the soil over to bury weeds and debris and loosen any compacted ground. At the same time organic matter – rotted manure or garden compost, for example – is mixed into the soil to improve the structure and fertility for next year's crops.

The freshly dug soil is then left as clods over winter to weather. In spring a seedbed or a level surface suitable for planting can be made with a cultivator, rake and treading.

In nature plants grow well enough without any digging and it is well known that the no-dig method can be highly successful. Since hand digging actually damages soil as it disrupts the microorganisms and earthworms that contribute very much to the fertility of soil, no digging should on the face of it be better than digging regimes. However, many gardeners find the good effects of digging are well worth the extra effort and inconvenience compared to no digging.

In an ideal world soil would not be dug and the ground would be left covered with vegetation or crop debris over winter. But this is not always possible as it is difficult to make the ground ready for sowing and planting in spring at the right time and slugs can be encouraged by the shelter provided.

Other options to **control weeds** and keep the soil covered over winter, which is highly beneficial to soils, include covering with plastic sheets (ideally black) to control weed growth or planting cover crops such as rye that will suppress weeds, scavenge nutrients and improve the soil when incorporated in the spring.

**Adding manure** in autumn, whether dug in or as a mulch, risks losing nutrients and possibly causing pollution as nutrients are washed out over winter by the rain.

Alternatively, particularly on light sandy well-drained soils, incorporating manure in the spring will avoid this loss as will using the manure as a mulch to **growing crops later.**

Another point to bear in mind when digging is that the ground should not be left **too fluffy or loose.** This is a particular problem in spring and when using a rotavator. Any tendency to looseness can be counteracted by treading or rolling.

**Wet soil** should never be worked nor even walked upon. It has little strength and can be compacted and spread very easily. This destroys the soil structure, reducing its ability to retain water and nutrients and allowing roots to penetrate.

# Potting media

Garden soil is too poorly structured to work well in pots so instead gardeners use a carefully formulated material commonly called potting compost but perhaps more accurately termed 'growing medium' as it is not actually a compost at all. Compost is in fact a poor growing medium as it lacks sufficient air spaces. Growing medium is composed of a mixture of various minerals and organic materials that will fulfil the important functions that a plant needs when it's taken from its natural environment of soil and grown in a pot.

**Roots need water** and they also need air. A well-formulated growing medium will have many spaces between the constituent particles that water flows through quickly to drain away. These will fill with air once water has drained and there will then be sufficient air in the medium for good root growth. Like all living things roots need oxygen. However plenty of air risks drought as water runs through too quickly. In the opposite case of a fine-textured growing medium water flows through slowly so there's plenty of water for plants for a long time after watering, but there might also be very few air spaces and plant roots are at risk of drowning. In winter plants use very little water and the root zone may remain saturated for long periods which is potentially very damaging.

Well-formulated **growing media** will have small and medium-sized pores which hold water and also sufficient larger pores which drain quickly after watering. The larger pores allow air to reach the roots and the other pores retain moisture in between waterings. Garden soil may well have about 50–60 percent of its volume as air-filled spaces. A good growing medium will have 75–95 percent of its volume filled with air and many pores will be much bigger than those in garden soils.

At the opposite end of water demand, succulents and cacti naturally need a **very fast-draining compost** as they have no great need and indeed won't tolerate moisture.

Growing media are formulated for particular purposes; hanging baskets require fine-textured medium that holds much water. Drainage in hanging baskets is almost by definition very fast and thorough.

Some plants, trees and shrubs for example, grow for several years in their pots and they need a compost with plenty of air spaces because as growing medium ages it rots and gradually the air spaces become smaller and smaller.

# Feeding

In nature plants grow pretty well without fertilizers or manures and this is often because they have associated fungal partners called mycorrhiza that in exchange for some sugars from the plants gather water and nutrients from the soil and transfer these to the plant. Also natural soil is rich in organisms that fix nitrogen from the atmosphere and slowly degrade soil minerals to release nutrients. Plants grow in self-sustaining partnerships. Very little is lost from natural systems as they are not harvested as such.

It is quite otherwise in gardens. Cultivation and fertilizers prevent mycorrhiza form functioning, soil organisms are less prolific in cultivated soils and plant partnerships are disrupted. Much material is harvested whether for consumption as with fruit and vegetables or in the course of making a beautiful garden with flowerbeds and lawns.

The best results in gardens usually result from adding to fertility, ideally by manures (p196) but also by fertilizers which increase growth rates and yields of produce and flowers. Research suggest that good plants can be grown by fertilizers alone but practical gardeners are likely to find that good soil management and careful manuring and mulching are required in addition to fertilizers.

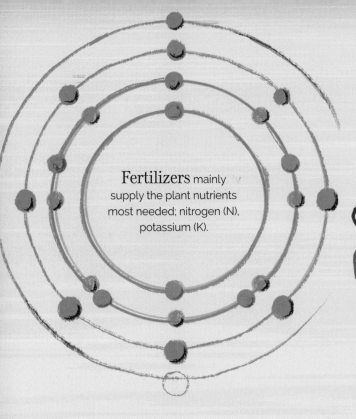

**Fertilizers** mainly supply the plant nutrients most needed; nitrogen (N), potassium (K).

**Other nutrients** are used in quite large quantities but are seldom in deficit; calcium (Ca), magnesium (Mg) and sulphur (S). Phosphorus (P) is not needed in great quantities but there is very little in natural soils so adding more is often advisable.

Investing in a **laboratory soil analysis** every five years or before making a new garden will give a very accurate idea of the soil nutrient status and allow fertilizers to be applied without waste to correct any deficiency before planting.

**Fertilizers** can be organic and derived from natural substances such as seaweed, poultry manure or wastes from abattoirs and food-processing activities such as bone and fish meal.

**Granular**, pelleted or powdered fertilizers are generally used for open ground and the more expensive liquid fertilizers reserved for containers and pot plants.

# Manuring

Adding extra **organic matter** to soil is broadly referred to as manuring as the main materials used are manure and bedding, from farms and stables. These are waste products that are relatively cheap.

**In some regions** composted municipal wastes or even sewage are available. These can be cost-effective but the former should be free of plastic and glass materials and the latter should be accompanied by a copy of a laboratory analysis report showing it is free of pathogens and heavy metals.

**Mushroom compost** is also often offered and is a good manure but tends to be alkaline and should be avoided where acid-loving lime-hating plants such as heathers are to be grown.

Manuring adds to the organic matter of the soil, improving its texture and making it easier to work. In truth this benefit lasts only **three years** as most organic matter rots quite fast and is not incorporated into the resilient long-term organic fraction of the soil. Therefore when planning vegetable gardens in particular manuring at least every three years is desirable.

Manures also add **nutrients** to the soil. Although the nutrient content is very low, typically 2–3 percent nitrogen, phosphorus, potassium and magnesium, large amounts, typically 5–10kg/11–22lb per sq m/yd of manures are added to the soil and in many cases this will supply all that crops require.

Adding manures increases the **water-holding capacity** of the soil both by absorbing water on its own account and by improving the soil structure, adding more pores from which plant roots can suck moisture.

Manures can **contain weed seeds** and also possibly plant diseases if the beasts were given fodder containing club root (brassicas), rhizomania (beet) or sclertinia spores (a wide range of hosts). In practice the risk is outweighed by the benefit.

**Weedkiller residues** can occur in some manures from animals fed on treated forages and assurances from the farmer or stable-owner should be sought on this point.

Manures can be **tested at home** by mixing the manure and good-quality potting media 50:50 and sowing four broad bean seeds in each of two 15cm/6in pots. A control of two other pots filled only with potting medium and bean seeds is made at the same time. If, after incubation in a warm sunny place, the beans from the manure mixture pot fail to emerge or are smaller and more distorted than the ones in the growing medium only control, then weedkiller is highly likely to be present.

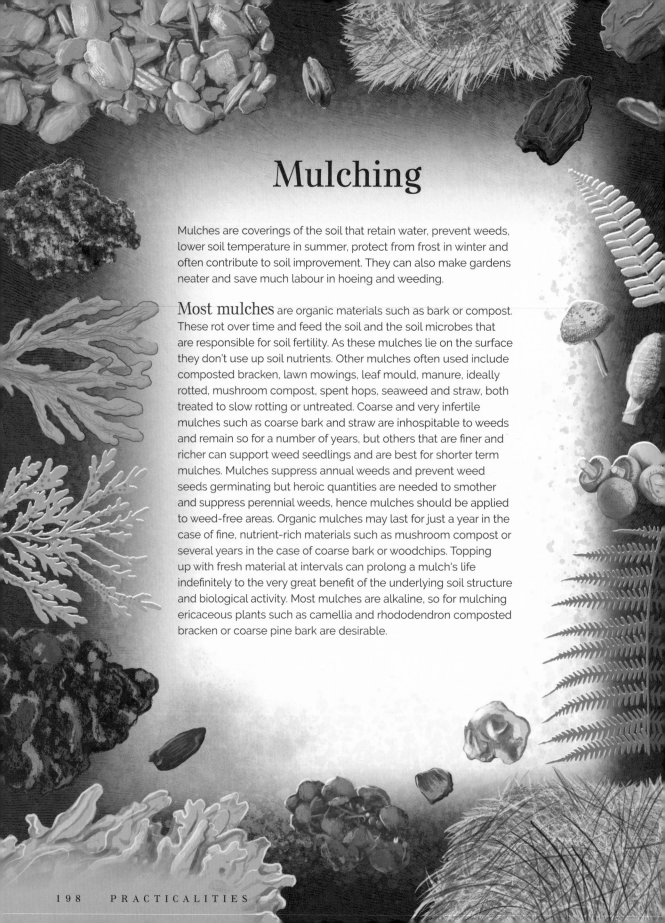

# Mulching

Mulches are coverings of the soil that retain water, prevent weeds, lower soil temperature in summer, protect from frost in winter and often contribute to soil improvement. They can also make gardens neater and save much labour in hoeing and weeding.

Most mulches are organic materials such as bark or compost. These rot over time and feed the soil and the soil microbes that are responsible for soil fertility. As these mulches lie on the surface they don't use up soil nutrients. Other mulches often used include composted bracken, lawn mowings, leaf mould, manure, ideally rotted, mushroom compost, spent hops, seaweed and straw, both treated to slow rotting or untreated. Coarse and very infertile mulches such as coarse bark and straw are inhospitable to weeds and remain so for a number of years, but others that are finer and richer can support weed seedlings and are best for shorter term mulches. Mulches suppress annual weeds and prevent weed seeds germinating but heroic quantities are needed to smother and suppress perennial weeds, hence mulches should be applied to weed-free areas. Organic mulches may last for just a year in the case of fine, nutrient-rich materials such as mushroom compost or several years in the case of coarse bark or woodchips. Topping up with fresh material at intervals can prolong a mulch's life indefinitely to the very great benefit of the underlying soil structure and biological activity. Most mulches are alkaline, so for mulching ericaceous plants such as camellia and rhododendron composted bracken or coarse pine bark are desirable.

Non-organic mulches can deal with perennial weeds. These are biodegradable plastics derived from maize, black sheet materials of plastic film or woven plastic, or special paper. They are not pretty but can be covered with bark, gravel or other decorative materials. They are especially useful in the fruit and vegetable garden. Rain reaches plants through the holes cut in the mulch for sowing or planting or can pass through permeable materials such as woven or nonwoven porous plastics. Even the biodegradable mulches will do little to improve the soil, though black mulches absorb sunlight and warm the underlying soil which is very beneficial for hot-season crops such as tomatoes and courgettes, for example. However, black sheets get so hot that some plants can be burnt and for these, strawberries for example, a white-faced, black-underside mulching sheet has been developed. White mulches are used in greenhouses to reflect light back up into the crop canopy. Biodegradable materials are best for short-term crops and are clearly much more environmentally sustainable than plastic materials.

Organic mulches are best applied in late winter to lock in winter rains and prevent the spring flush of annual weeds. A minimum thickness of 5cm/2in is required and 8cm/3in is more reliable. Mulch should not touch the stems and trunks of plants as this may lead to rotting. In summer the soil is often too dry and in autumn and winter the soil can be too wet or indeed too dry in certain years. Winter rains will also wash out the nutrient content of some mulches, leading to waste and potential pollution. Sheet mulches, are applied from spring before sowing or planting of annual crops or before weed growth in fruit and other perennial plants.

# Making compost

In composting the trick is to mix carbon-rich materials that also keep the compost open with nitrogen-rich materials to provide the **microbes** and **fungi** that do the rotting with nitrogen to help them break down the resistant carbon-rich materials.

Garden compost is ready when it is dark, crumbly and soil-like.

**Organic materials** from clippings to shoots from pruning will eventually rot if moist and warm enough. Some materials such as sawdust, straw and prunings are very rich in carbon but low in nitrogen and rot very slowly. Others such as kitchen wastes rot fast because they contain little carbon and much nitrogen.

**Rotting** occurs in air-rich and in airless, or anaerobic, conditions. Garden composting is best done aerobically. Materials that set in a soggy mass such as lawn mowings will rot slowly and anaerobically unless opened up by strawy materials.

**Generally** a mix of 50–75 percent parts by volume of carbon-rich and 25–50 percent of nitrogen-rich materials will give good results. Really woody material such as prunings are best disposed of by burning or, better, shredding, for use as mulch. Autumn fallen leaves are also quite resistant to rotting and if available large amounts are best left to rot on their own to produce leaf mould.

**Soft** green wastes predominate in most gardens, but carbon-rich straw, cardboard or even scrunched-up balls of newspaper can be used to get the desired balance. If it happens that strawy dry wastes predominate, activators, essentially nitrogen fertilizers, or pelleted poultry manure, can be added to achieve the required balance.

**Composting** can generate high temperatures if a large mass is made in one session. Hot composting is highly desirable as rotting is fast and diseased materials, pests and weeds are destroyed.

**Turning,** or in other words extracting all the rotting material and then putting it back in the bin all mixed up with any dry patches wetted and strawy material incorporated into slimy soggy areas, will greatly speed up composting and often induces useful heat.

# Pruning

Pruning is essentially the removal of plant parts – shoots, stems and even, rarely, roots – to manipulate the plant's growth into desired shapes and activities such as flowering. Although soft plants including vegetables and flowers are often pinched and side-shoots removed and cut back at various times and the end of the season, pruning is mostly concerned with woody plants; climbers, shrubs and trees. In practice trees are too large to prune to a great extent and climbers, except many clematis and roses, are too tangled to be easy subjects for pruning other than shearing.

Pruning involves **predicting** how plants will grow afterwards and if it is not likely to be beneficial replacing plants may be necessary instead. Typically, unwise planting of oversize shrubs and trees results in large plants that are pruned heavily to make them fit available space. They often look unsightly and fail to flower or fruit. Sad to say replacement rather than pruning is the remedy in these cases.

Pruning may be a **regular activity** as in the pruning of fruit bushes or it may be occasional when a large shrub or tree is cut back to shape and renovate it.

A **good pruning book** is invaluable and as pruning has been much the same for decades if not longer a secondhand book is adequate. However, in broad terms there are three pruning methods.

Shrubs that flower in **spring and early summer,** including the much-loved forsythia, philadelphus and weigela for example, are pruned after flowering, removing about one spent flowering stem in three to near ground level.

Those that flower from **late summer to autumn** such as caryopteris and deciduous ceanothus are pruned in early spring to induce the vigorous shoots which carry flowers in their first season from late summer.

**Evergreen plants** do not need regular pruning but can be reduced by pruning in spring before growth starts or, in the case of spring-flowering shrubs such as camellia and choisya, after flowering.

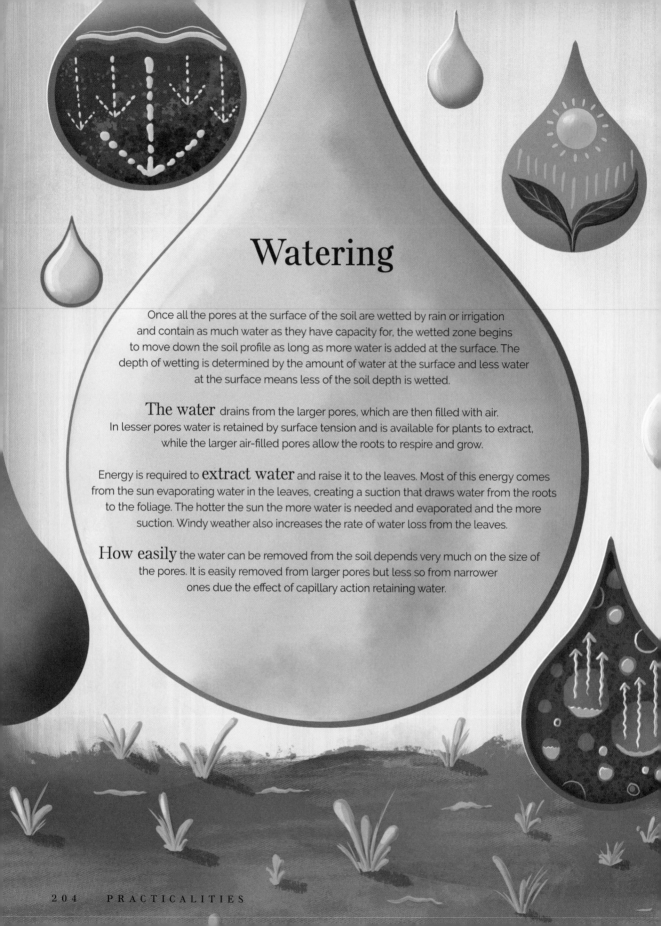

# Watering

Once all the pores at the surface of the soil are wetted by rain or irrigation and contain as much water as they have capacity for, the wetted zone begins to move down the soil profile as long as more water is added at the surface. The depth of wetting is determined by the amount of water at the surface and less water at the surface means less of the soil depth is wetted.

The water drains from the larger pores, which are then filled with air. In lesser pores water is retained by surface tension and is available for plants to extract, while the larger air-filled pores allow the roots to respire and grow.

Energy is required to extract water and raise it to the leaves. Most of this energy comes from the sun evaporating water in the leaves, creating a suction that draws water from the roots to the foliage. The hotter the sun the more water is needed and evaporated and the more suction. Windy weather also increases the rate of water loss from the leaves.

How easily the water can be removed from the soil depends very much on the size of the pores. It is easily removed from larger pores but less so from narrower ones due the effect of capillary action retaining water.

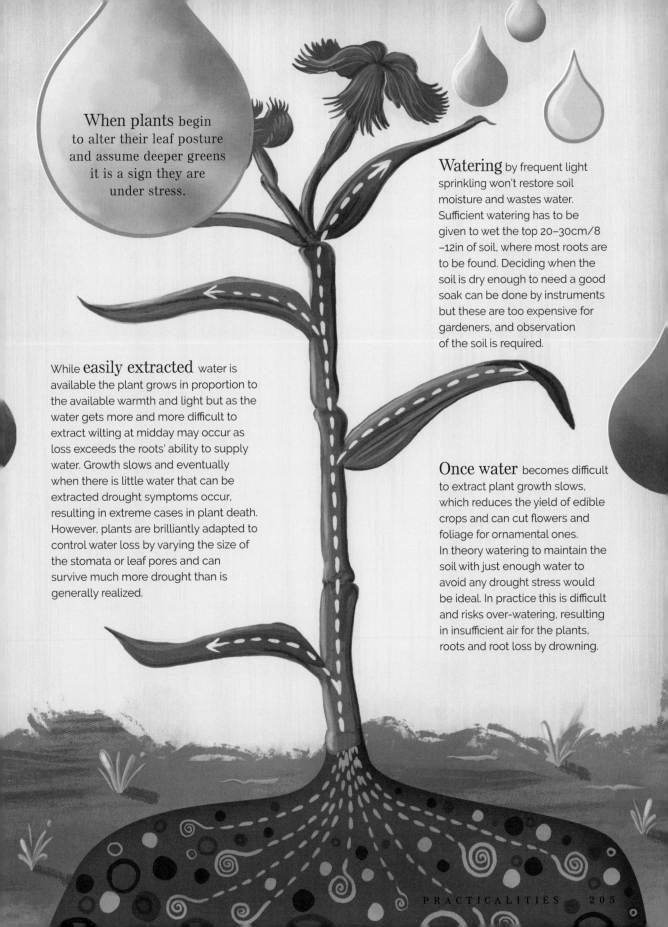

When plants begin to alter their leaf posture and assume deeper greens it is a sign they are under stress.

**Watering** by frequent light sprinkling won't restore soil moisture and wastes water. Sufficient watering has to be given to wet the top 20–30cm/8 –12in of soil, where most roots are to be found. Deciding when the soil is dry enough to need a good soak can be done by instruments but these are too expensive for gardeners, and observation of the soil is required.

While **easily extracted** water is available the plant grows in proportion to the available warmth and light but as the water gets more and more difficult to extract wilting at midday may occur as loss exceeds the roots' ability to supply water. Growth slows and eventually when there is little water that can be extracted drought symptoms occur, resulting in extreme cases in plant death. However, plants are brilliantly adapted to control water loss by varying the size of the stomata or leaf pores and can survive much more drought than is generally realized.

**Once water** becomes difficult to extract plant growth slows, which reduces the yield of edible crops and can cut flowers and foliage for ornamental ones. In theory watering to maintain the soil with just enough water to avoid any drought stress would be ideal. In practice this is difficult and risks over-watering, resulting in insufficient air for the plants, roots and root loss by drowning.

# Weeds

Weeds are extraordinary plants brilliantly adapted to invading cultivated land. They mimic the life cycles of the plants grown in gardens so that bedding borders and vegetable gardens full of annual plants are infested with annual weeds such as nettles and fat hen, while perennial borders and fruit gardens are vulnerable to perennial weeds such as bindweed and ground elder. Lawn weeds are able to cope with the mower blades by pressing themselves close to the soil, daisies and plantains being classic examples.

Weeds are also very **well adapted** to seizing opportunities to invade any open uncropped soil by producing vast quantities of seeds that drift on the breeze, groundsel for example, or by highly dormant seeds such as those of poppies that can lie inactive but alive in the soil for decades. Most buried weed seed however only survives a few years.

Weed control is in fact weed management – it is almost impossible to eradicate them as they recur whenever opportunity arises. However, managing the garden to limit weed opportunities the labour of weed control is reduced.

The best **weed control** is not to have weeds so when making a new garden the very greatest care should be taken not to import infested manure or soil, and to remove and discard growing media from bought in plants and wash the soil from bare root plants before planting.

As weeds are so **highly adapted** to occupying uncultivated ground, avoid bare soil. Sowing a thick quick-growing leafy cover crop such as mustard or ryegrass on any bare soil can exclude weeds, and the cover crop is dug in or composted later.

**Digging** to bury weeds and pick out pernicious roots is an excellent, if laborious, way of eliminating perennial and living annual weeds but if dormant seeds are present they will be brought to the surface to germinate later. Daylight and the fluctuating temperatures found near the soil surface trigger weed seeds to germinate.

**Mulches** are a particularly good way of preventing weeds (p198-9), not least after digging, when any weed seedlings will be unable to reach the light.

**Weeds** must not be allowed to flower and set seed at almost any cost. Hoeing and hand weeding are highly effective in good weather at controlling low weed populations. In wet conditions weeds can be harder to control.

Although farmers use selective **weed killers** or herbicides to prevent or remove weeds from a wide range of crops these are only offered for lawn weed control in gardens. Lawn weedkillers are plant hormone analogues that affect broad-leaved plants and not grasses. Each active chemical ingredient controls a limited spectrum of weeds so lawn weedkillers contain a mix of active herbicide molecules to eliminate almost any lawn weed.

# How to plant new climbers, shrubs & trees

Climbers, shrubs and trees are often difficult to establish. Establishment is the period from planting to when the plant roots out into the surrounding soil and becomes much less vulnerable to misfortune, particularly insufficient water.

If plants have **not established** within two years of planting the outlook is poor and replacement is often the best remedy. Even if such plants are alive they may well be 'checked' in their growth, a condition that trees in particular seldom fully recover from. Happily most garden centres now offer two – or even five – year guarantees so that when this happens seeking a replacement involves no extra cost, although the loss of two years' growth is inevitable.

## Lack of water can result from dry weather and failure to appreciate when and how much water is required by plants while they are establishing.

Good planting **technique** goes a long way to avoiding establishment problems. Although container-grown plants can be planted at any season, autumn and winter planting are best. Bareroot and 'rootballed' plants are only offered in autumn and winter.

Preparing **the site** with cultivation to eliminate weeds and compacted soil that might impair drainage is the first step. Adding manure in a broad area is helpful but adding manure or other organic matter to the planting hole can lead to the soil shrinking as the manure rots, causing excessively deep planting.

Prepare a **planting hole** deep enough to accommodate the plant and considerably wider than the root ball. In grassed areas this might involve removing a circle of turf at least 1m/3¼ft in diameter. Square planting holes are better than round ones as they can reduce the risk of roots circulating and potentially strangling the tree or at least failing to explore surrounding soil.

After **soaking roots** in a bucket of water for about an hour place the plant in the planting hole, with the roots just below the soil surface. If a stake is required this should go in before planting.

**The soil** from the planting hole can then be replaced and the ground firmly made level.

**Watering** is now key, but the need will not arise until spring or early summer. A little bank of earth around the newly planted subject will allow water to be added in sufficient quantity to soak deeply.

As the **wetness** of the surface is no guide to depth of wetting uncertain gardeners should use their trowel to inspect a few hours after watering to ensure the rootball is wetted.

Weeds suck up much **moisture** and are ideally prevented by mulching or, failing that, by hoeing or in severe cases direct-contact herbicide sprays.

When strong **new growth** is seen the plant can be considered to be successfully established.

# Making new plants
# from seed

Seeds are the most economical way of growing new plants but usually being small seeds produce only small seedlings that can take some years to reach a useful size.

Seeds almost **always arise** from sexual reproduction and there will be variations in individuals in a seed-grown population. There is particularly little variation in hybrid seed. Home-saved seed can be especially variable, but while variability might be undesirable on a farm or nursery it is often an asset in the garden.

Seed can be **bought**, or **collected** (with permission) from other gardens or, within strict limits, from the wild. Collecting seed from the wild abroad is especially problematic as local laws may place especially tight controls on seed collecting and unless done with a bona fide group it is best avoided. Plant societies often offer seed distribution schemes at a very modest cost to their own members, with in many cases a discount to those who contribute seed.

A **propagating area** to germinate seeds is well worth preparing where a clean table can be used to sow seeds into fresh growing medium that is sufficiently fine to allow seeds to have close contact with the media, into pots and pans and trays that have been washed and ideally dipped in disinfectant. A heated propagator is worth using for most of the year in cooler regions.

**When sowing** the medium should be firm and level and just deep enough to bury the seeds. Fine vermiculite is often used for this purpose as light will pass through it and it is unlikely to pack down and impede seedling emergence. Very fine seeds often have a high light requirement and can be sown on the medium surface, with the pan then covered with clingfilm. Cyclamen seed needs darkness to germinate and covering the pan with aluminium foil will provide the necessary conditions.

**Seeds need warmth** to germinate, typically 18–25°C/64–77°F, and are vulnerable to rot if kept too cool or wet. Seedlings too need warmth and are extremely vulnerable to the disease 'damping off' as they emerge. In the absence of fungicides the only way of dealing with this is scrupulous hygiene and careful attention to heat, humidity and watering.

# Making new plants from cuttings

Many plants possess the ability to generate new plants from portions of the plant such as roots, leaves and most commonly stems. The length of stem taken and used for propagation is called a cutting. Leaf and root cuttings are also used.

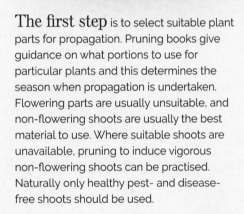

**The first step** is to select suitable plant parts for propagation. Pruning books give guidance on what portions to use for particular plants and this determines the season when propagation is undertaken. Flowering parts are usually unsuitable, and non-flowering shoots are usually the best material to use. Where suitable shoots are unavailable, pruning to induce vigorous non-flowering shoots can be practised. Naturally only healthy pest- and disease-free shoots should be used.

**Young green shoots**, by definition this season's growth, taken from a very wide range of deciduous plants, in early summer often have excellent potential for rooting. They must not be ragged or crushed when cut and an extremely sharp knife is ideal. Cuttings of green material are very soft and dry out extremely quickly. They are therefore usually on the small side (10cm/4in) and kept in a highly humid atmosphere to prevent wilting. Wilted cuttings cannot photosynthesize and will therefore soon run out of nutrients. Cuttings taken in the early morning will be fully turgid and less liable to wilt.

An important
point is to make the
lower cut just below a leaf
joint (node) as this is where
plant hormones involved in
rooting are highest. Dipping
cuttings in rooting powder
or liquid that contains
suitable hormones is
worthwhile.

Heating from the base is often useful and a differential between a warm rooting zone and cooler aerial parts is helpful to rooting. Once roots form the cuttings can be exposed to increased airflow and placed in a warm bright place to grow until they have enough roots for potting into individual pots.

Cuttings **form roots** in response to darkness and moisture, so the lower half of the cutting is stripped of leaves and gently inserted with the aid of a dibber into a rooting medium that is typically half grit or perlite and half multipurpose potting medium. Very soft growing tips are also removed as these wilt very easily indeed. It is then covered with clear or white plastic to prevent drying out and placed in good but not scorching light.

Later in **summer** and **early autumn** semi-ripe cuttings can be used for many evergreen plants such as hebe and lavender and a few deciduous ones including berberis. Here the shoots are less soft, less inclined to wilt and also slower to root. They are taken in the same way as softwood cuttings but are easier to handle. The lower part of the cutting is quite hard, but the top is still soft. The cuttings are a little longer than soft ones, about 10–15cm/4–6in, and again inserted into a rooting medium of grit or perlite and multipurpose medium.

# Easy ways of making new plants

Taking cuttings is an excellent way of making new plants but it does require care and considerable input of time. Easier ways are often very useful on a garden scale although perhaps not so practical for nursery growers.

**Many plants**, coleus and fuchsia for example, root happily in a jar of water. To keep the water wholesome it is often a good idea to wrap the jar in aluminium foil. Such jars are by tradition kept on a windowsill. When plenty of roots have formed the plants are potted into growing medium. The 'water roots' seldom survive long in the growing medium but the plant is in a state where it can make roots rapidly and it soon sends out roots into the surrounding medium.

**Layering** is a much neglected form of propagation that is highly reliable and requires little finesse. A low-growing shoot is bent down to soil or below soil level and covered in earth, perhaps mounded if necessary. It can be held in place with a brick or more elegantly a wire staple, perhaps made from a clothes hanger. A good extra trick is to give the bent stem a slight twist where it is at its lowest point. This wounds the plant tissue and encourages rooting. The 'layer' is then left to root. Layering is best done in spring and by autumn the shoot is well rooted and can be severed from the parent and planted out.

**Blackberries** and hybrid berries layer themselves as they ramp along. Their tips root where they touch the soil and a new plant forms that in turn sends out a shoot that will eventually root and so on. Making more hybrid berry and blackberry plants is especially easy.

**Climbers** can be multiple layered where the long stems of clematis and honeysuckle are laid along the ground and buried at intervals. A new plant arises at each point where the stem is buried. This is called serpentine layering.

Most **popluar plants** from agapanthus to verbena can be propagated by divison. Lift the clump from the soil with a fork and, using a knife or spade, take individaul plantlets from the edges of the plant where the growth is most healthy. Summer-flowering plants are best divided in autumn and winter whenever the soil is dry enough or can be left to spring. Spring-flowering plants can be done in summer after flowering as this is when they make new roots. In fact there is no reason to be patient – using a knife and a delicate touch, plantlets with roots attached can be gently separated from clumps of summer flowers and potted up.

# Staking

Tall annual and herbaceous plants tend to collapse under heavy rain and wind and need support. Showy plants with outsize flower heads or spikes need supports for their massive blooms that are even heavier when wet after rain. Dahlias and delphiniums are examples of these. Smaller modern gardens tend to be shaded and plants tend to be drawn up in shade, becoming tall and lax.

It is true that shorter plants are available but the drama of tall flowers at the back of borders is hard to forego and for cut flowers tall plants with long stems are needed. In any case even shorter plants can flop onto lawns and paths and need restraining.

Unfortunately once plants have fallen it is very difficult to get them up again and supported in a pleasing manner. Therefore staking or supporting before plants grow tall is advisable.

Cutting gardens can be more functional than decorative and wire mesh (15cm/6in) placed on the ground can be slid up poles spaced at intervals so the mesh rises with the plants. This low-maintenance supporting method also works well for dahlias, delphiniums and other decorative plants with large blooms. Here the mesh is well hidden by foliage and the posts can be painted black so they sink into the background. Tall canes and string can also be used for individual plants, or where heavy plants are involved, wire mesh cylinders to hold the plant in place and secured with several vertical canes are possible. String can cut into stems and to avoid this a soft string loosely tied is used. Bamboo canes and string are perhaps best consigned to the vegetable garden.

**Wire mesh** is a little too workmanlike for an ornamental border, although it can be discreetly used at the back of borders for top-heavy plants. There are, however, sturdy circular plastic-coated metal grid or spiral supports especially made for bushy top-heavy plants such as peonies that can be raised as the plant grows. More useful are plastic-coated wire circles, linkable stakes and Y-shaped supports that are easy to insert and to store over winter. As the plant grows they can be lifted higher in the soil but they are available too in a range of heights to match garden plants of different stature.

It is best to err on the **short side** when choosing supports. If plants grow unexpectedly tall it is easier to insert some taller supports than try to push down ones that stand above the plants in an unsightly way. Many metal supports are ornamented with metal-work, flowers and birds, for example, at the top – an advantage of these is that the metalwork is built-in eye protection. It is wise to use plastic caps for canes as uncapped these can easily give a dangerous jab in the eye.

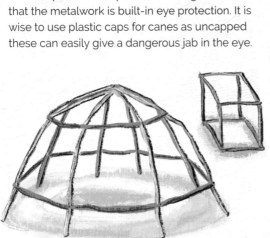

**Sweet peas** for cutting can be trained to vertical rods or canes and side shoots removed. However, for general use a wigwam will support sweetpeas well.

**Twiggy sticks** can also be woven and twined to make domes and rough cubes with an open structure through which plants can grow. By using suitable lengths of stick quite large structures can be made. These might be time-consuming to make each year but they are objects of natural beauty that are often very worthwhile additions to gardens.

# Problems

Plants being living organisms, they are vulnerable to infection by diseases and infestation by pests. It is inevitable that these will be encountered sooner or later.

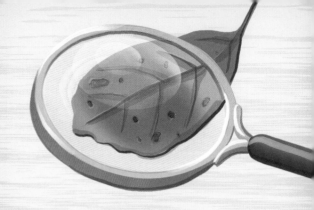

The best way to **avoid problems** is not to let them in. New plants should be carefully inspected for foliar pests and for leaf spots, moulds or pustules. When the plant to buy has been selected one last check of the roots can be made.

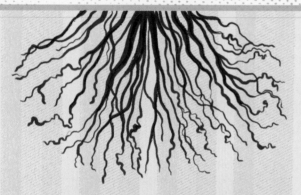

Avoid plants where the **roots are dark**, brittle and rotted as this indicates poor watering practice and quite possibly fungal root diseases.

**Plants** from well-meaning friends are not always what they should be in terms of problems and discreetly binning such gifts is often wise.

It is **worth noting** that many disease-resistant or at least tolerant cultivars are offered and these offer the best way of controlling diseases and, less commonly, pests.

**Pests** are often highly mobile and fly in from several miles away having an uncanny ability to detect host plants from afar. Covering young plants with fleece or insect-proof mesh is good practice.

When pests are **seen outdoors** a decision has to be made to treat or not. If they are not numerous and not doing much damage they can be controlled by picking off or blasting with the hose pipe and any survivors left to natural predators and parasites.

An **insecticide** can be used to eliminate many pests. Insecticides based on oils or soaps (fatty acids) and that work by physical action leave no residues and are useful for edible crops.

**Holes** often arise on leaves and slugs and snails are by far the commonest cause. Their presence is indicated by slime trails or they can more easily be found at night when they tend to feed.

**Wilting plants** or ones with dieback of the foliage indicate a soil or root problem. Vine weevils are a common cause in pot plants and outdoor plants with thick fleshy roots such as bergenias and hosta. Prevention with a nematode drench ideally in autumn and less usefully in spring can prevent these soil pests.

Other **fungal diseases** cause moulds and leaf spots on foliage. Fungicides can prevent or limit some fungal leaf pathogens such as rose blackspot and powdery mildew, but many other diseases cannot be treated.

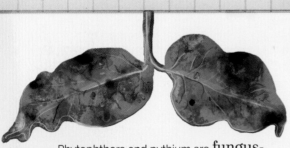

Phytophthora and pythium are **fungus-like organisms** that cause root rots, particularly in wet soil. They can be prevented by good drainage, but once they strike, typically by progressive destruction of the plant from one side, replacement is called for.

# Glossary

**Accelerator** Any substance used to speed up the decomposition of organic matter in garden compost.

**Acid soil** Soil with a pH below 7. See also pH.

**Aeration** Loosening the soil to increase its permeability to water and air.

**Alkaline soil** Soil with a pH above 7, notably soils derived from limestone. See also pH.

**Annual** A plant that completes its life cycle in one growing season.

**Aphid** Also known as blackfly or greenfly, aphids are small insects that suck sap from plants and can cause extensive damage.

**Bare-root** A plant sold with little or no soil around its roots, ready for planting.

**Beneficial insect** An insect that is useful to the gardener, for example by pollinating flowers, destroying harmful insects or breaking down plant material in the soil and releasing its nutrients.

**Biennial** A plant that germinates and develops foliage and roots during its first year, then produces flowers and seeds in the second year before dying at the end of the growing season.

**Blight** A fungal or bacterial disease that causes rapid, extensive discoloration, followed by death of the plant tissue.

**Bolting** Flowering or producing seed prematurely, usually caused by hot weather or lack of water. Removing flower heads from leaf crops such as lettuce discourages bolting.

**Bract** A modified leaf, which is usually small but is sometimes large and brightly coloured, such as in poinsettia.

**Chlorosis** Yellowing of leaves caused by iron deficiency in lime-rich soils, disease or lack of light.

**Cloche** A small translucent glass or plastic cover for protecting outdoor plants from frost and warming their environment to encourage growth.

**Colonization** The movement of plant species into new areas by natural means.

**Compost** Humus made by allowing vegetative matter to decompose in a compost heap or bin; also, specifically formulated mixtures for raising seedlings and young plants in containers.

**Cultivar** A plant variety produced in cultivation by selective breeding.

**Damping off** A fungal disease that causes emerging seedlings to collapse.

**Deadhead** To remove spent flowerheads in order to encourage further flowering.

**Dibber** A pointed wooden tool for making holes in the ground in which seeds, seedlings or bulbs can be planted.

**Dieback** Death of shoots, branches, or roots, usually starting at the tips.

**Division** A method of plant propagation where the plant is divided into two or more clumps to produce extra plants that will be genetically identical.

**Drill** A shallow furrow made in the soil in which to sow seeds.

**Earthing-up** Piling soil up around the base of a plant – particularly potatoes, to encourage yield and exclude light which would cause them to become green and inedible.

**Espalier** A form of training where a tree or shrub is grown flat on a trellis or wall.

**Ericaceous** A term describing plants from the family *Ericaceae* as well as the growing media and fertilizers suitable for them. Ericaceous plants are lime-haters and require acid soil.

**Etiolation** Long, weak, pale yellow plant stems caused by lack of light in their growing environment.

**$F_1$ hybrid** A plant bred by crossing two parent plants that have been self-pollinated over several generations to preserve desired characteristics and create what is known as a pure line.

**Foliar feeding** Applying diluted soluble fertilizer directly to the leaves of a plant.

**Force** To bring a plant into early growth by providing it with extra warmth.

**Fungicide** A chemical control for fungal diseases.

**Genus** A group of related but distinct species that forms a family.

**Germination** The sprouting stage of a seed.

**Grafting** Propagating a plant by uniting a shoot or bud of one plant with the trunk, branch or roots of another.

**Green manure** A crop that is grown and then dug into the soil to return organic matter and nitrogen to it.

Clover and comfrey are commonly used for this purpose.

**Half-hardy** A plant that may survive a few degrees of frost but is killed at lower temperatures.

**Hardening-off** Gradually exposing seedlings started indoors to outdoor conditions before transplanting.

**Hardy** A plant that can tolerate frost.

**Heeling in** Temporary burying of a plant's roots to prevent them drying out until a permanent site is prepared.

**Herbaceous perennial** A plant that dies back in the winter and regrows from the crown in spring.

**Hybrid** The offspring of two plants of different species.

**Inflorescence** The complete flower head of a plant.

**Insecticide** A chemical control for insect pests.

**Invasive** Growing vigorously and out-competing other plants.

**Layering** A method of propagating a plant by fastening down a shoot from which roots will form while still attached to the parent plant.

**Loam** A soil that has a mixture of sand, silt and clay, ideal for many plants.

**Maiden** A one-year-old tree, sold as feathered (with side shoots that will form the main branches) or unfeathered (a single stem with no sideshoots).

**Microclimate** The climate of a very small or restricted area, especially when this differs from the climate of the surrounding area.

**Nematode** A microscopic roundworm, usually in the soil, which may carry disease. Others are beneficial parasites of insect pests and can be bought for the purpose as a natural form of pest control.

**Node** The part of a plant's stem from which one or more leaves grow.

**Offset** A new shoot that forms in a leaf axil or at the base of a plant.

**Open-pollinated seed** Seed produced from natural, random pollination where the resulting plants may vary.

**Organic** Material originating from a living organism such as compost or manure; also describes plants grown without the use of synthetic chemicals.

**Perennial** A plant that lives at least two years and produces new foliage, flowers and seeds each growing season.

**pH** A measure of acidity or alkalinity. Values from 0 to 7 indicate acidity and those from 7 to 14 indicate alkalinity; 7 is neutral.

**Photosynthesis** A process of converting light energy, normally from the sun, into chemical energy that is used for plant growth.

**Pleach** To intertwine branches of trees or shrubs to form a hedge.

**Root-bound** A condition in which a plant's roots have completely filled its container and further growth is prevented until the plant is transferred to open ground or a larger container.

**Root cutting** A section of root used for vegetative propagation.

**Rootstock** A vigorous rooting plant upon which another (see Scion) is grafted.

**Runner** See Stolon.

**Scion** The shoot or bud of a plant which is grafted to the roots or stem of another. The scion produces the flowering or fruiting characteristics of the variety from which it has been taken.

**Species** Individuals within a genus capable of interbreeding. The species name (known as the specific epithet) is Latinized and follows the genus name.

**Stolon** A horizontal stem running along the soil surface and producing roots and leaves where its nodes contact the soil.

**Taproot** A sturdy central root from the plant's crown.

**Tender** A plant that cannot survive temperatures below 5°C/41°F.

**Variegation** Different-coloured marking in the leaves and sometimes the stems of plants.

**Vegetative propagation** Asexual reproduction of a plant where the offspring is the result of one parent and is genetically identical. It may occur by natural means (e.g. bulblets, offsets or stolons) or artificial means (e.g. cuttings, division, grafting or layering).

# Afterword from the author

Gardening or horticulture is science, art and craft. The craft starts with hands-on, physical activity from sowing seeds to pruning mature trees. In many ways this has hardly changed since ancient times. Roman authors and medieval prints describe and show tools, activities and concerns still recognisable today. There is something satisfying about following such an ancient tradition.

Science has certainly explored the basis of established practices and allowed them to be understood better, made more reliable and sometimes greatly improved. This enhances the rewards of gardening. Plant breeding is perhaps the most significant application of science and has resulted in a rich palette of plant material to work with.

Sometimes, however, we have over-reached and one of the most interesting current trends is stepping back from practices which are expensive and have the potential to do environmental harm. This is by no means a return to tradition, but an advance in knowledge and skills, just in a different direction. Self-sustaining plant communities, manipulating soil life to replace fertilizers, growing better plants with better understanding of how plants work, and improved pruning and management of trees for example. Gardening never stands still, not even in private gardens and certainly not in commercial horticulture. An interest in gardening is an interest for life.

Happily plants grow quite well with just a little science and craft, and tend to look good naturally if given half a chance. Design helps of course but it costs – a well-designed instant garden costs thousands, so it is no surprise that most gardeners develop their garden piecemeal trying this, moving that. No prizes for guessing how mine evolved.

I get satisfaction from and am energised by what is sometimes called 'low agriculture' that recreates the landscape of the Cranborne Chase, in south-west England, where I grew up; flower-rich downland, dappled woodlands, sunken lanes lined with spring bulbs, flowers and ferns between leafy hedges and neat, well-tended fields. Hands of nature and man artlessly combined is what I aspire to.

**Guy Barter**

# Afterword from the illustrator

In recent years the natural world has been taking on an ever increasing role in my work, so when the opportunity arose to be involved with this project it felt like perfect timing. Illustration is often about learning and interpreting new areas in which you have little direct experience, and this was especially true for me at the start of *Flora*. Having been immersed in Guy's writing for the past year I can now count myself as a passionate amateur gardener who holds a deep appreciation for the craft and what it can give to the human experience. I am sure that my involvement with *Flora* will profoundly influence my work for many years to come.

I try to combine collage, texture and digital techniques to create something that I hope is innovative and engaging, unmistakably modern but with a nod to historic styles. With *Flora*, the combination of classical floral illustration with modern digital painting was a perfect outlet for this.

I would like to thank Melissa Smith for having the faith in my ability to realise such a vast project. My wife Karen for her enduring support and my labrador Leo for the much needed rejuvenating woodland walks.

**Sam Falconer**

Creatively Independent

Brimming with creative inspiration, how-to projects and useful information to enrich
your everyday life, Quarto Knows is a favourite destination for those pursuing their interests
and passions. Visit our site and dig deeper with our books into your area of interest:
Quarto Creates, Quarto Cooks, Quarto Homes, Quarto Lives, Quarto Drives,
Quarto Explores, Quarto Gifts, or Quarto Kids.

First published in 2017 by Aurum Press, an imprint of The Quarto Group.
The Old Brewery, 6 Blundell Street, London N7 9BH, United Kingdom.
www.QuartoKnows.com

A catalogue record for this book is available from the British Library.

ISBN  978 1 78131 604 7
1 3 5 7 9 10 8 6 4 2
2017 2019 2021 2020 2018
Printed in China